get organized

find your keys & figure out life

Dee Bentley

ISBN-13: 978-0995078307 (Dee Bentley)

ISBN-10: 0995078300

All mentions of verses from the Holy Bible, New Testament and Old Testament Scriptures, are paraphrased by the author; any likeness to previously published paraphrases are unintended and accidental.

dedication

This book is dedicated to my wonderful family, and to my clients who allowed me to help them; they were really helping me.

Contents

1.

It Worked For Me—It Can Work For You

Have you ever noticed that feeling disorganized usually goes along with a sense of aimlessness in life? I was at that sticky place in my life. I kept thinking, 'If I could only get the house organized again, that would help me figure out the next step.' It worked. And I discovered how spiritual truth was related to areas of my home. How did I get stuck?

After my husband and I began a family, we felt a strong desire to homeschool our children. We jumped in and learned everything we could. Once we began, I gave it my all and we embraced the lifestyle. Seven years later, our youngest was born. When he was ten years old, he decided he wanted to attend school since he was lonely. His older siblings had moved out by then, which was also a difficult transition for me.

I flopped around for a while furthering my education and working, hoping to find a place I fit. Nothing seemed right. After two years, I seriously considered starting my own business, but what? I decided to get my house into shape. Bit by bit, as I organized my own home to reflect our life changes, a bright ribbon appeared, connecting each portion of my life. Suddenly, a plan became obvious. I wondered if this strategy could work for others?

There are many guides on organizing available, but organizing one's home and life works best when we do the hard work of relating our inner spiritual home to our outer homes: we welcome God into the process, untangle the past, accept the present, learn new systems, and go into the future walking in the Spirit.

I recommend you work through the book while you work through your home and heart. You could invite friends to join you on this journey: set the same day and time each week to meet, preferably without children so mums have a quiet time to recharge. Decide how long your meetings will be and stick to it. Consistency and predictability will make arranging child-care easier.

Every chapter has suggestions gained from twenty years of experience organizing in workplaces, within volunteer roles, my own home, and homes of others. At the end of each chapter you'll find a Heart Check section to help you examine your heart, a Prayer, and finally a Resources & Actions section. There are books to read, actions to put concepts into practice, and suggestions for group study.

While I recommend books throughout, most should be available through public libraries or as ebooks; alternatively, you could search similar topics on the Web. The Bible readings are available online. One site I used regularly is: www.biblegateway.com.

Journaling is a valuable tool to internalize the process. To assist you, I have left a Journal space at the end of each chapter. If you need more space, you could use an additional journal, or journal electronically on your computer or phone.

For simplicity, I refer to people as either he or she, though sections may apply to both genders. I've also used Canadian spelling, which I hope isn't distracting.

I believe God designed each of us for specific work, yet at times we lose our way. When we get stuck, we should do our best to get up, shake off hopelessness, and do the work in front of us. There we will find meaning in the menial and hope for the future.

heart check

Are you up for the challenge of organizing your home? Are you tired of your life and ready for change? When God is prompting us into a new chapter of life, it often begins with restlessness, a sudden change, or even a feeling of dissatisfaction. Change and growth are necessary parts of a relationship with our Living God.

My prayer for you—
Father God,
Please meet (dear reader) and help her through this journey. Thank You that You see her, and know all the hurts, joys and disappointments she's been through. Draw her close to you. Give her Your strength and bring her to a time of healing, refreshing, and new beginnings. You designed her

with a special purpose in mind. I know and trust that as she is faithful to You, You will reveal Yourself and Your purpose to her.
Amen

resources & actions

You

- Read Psalm 139. Consider how God wrote about all your days in His book.
- List in the Journal section your difficult life situations and transitions.
- Ask friends to join you on this journey. Working with others will help you stay motivated as you get organized.

Family

- Explain to your family that a new, exciting adventure is about to begin. Let them know that getting organized will take work, but it will make home better for all of you.

journal

2.

Where to Begin?

If you are feeling stuck in a place where life is missing purpose, you may feel like your home is out of control, too. You probably feel overwhelmed at the thought of tackling the messes you and others have made because you have cleaned a million times before and things haven't changed. What will be different this time? How can getting organized actually help you figure out life?

The truth is, you were probably an organized, focused person when it was just you. Then you were married and shortly after the messy children arrived with all their stuff which seems to grow exponentially with each passing year. It is one thing to organize yourself, but quite another to organize an entire family.

Because I had gone through some painful transition times, such as losing my ideal lifestyle, becoming an (almost) empty-nester, plus not finding a position where I fit, my own belongings were too difficult as a starting point.

Have you gone through some difficult transitions like moving to a new city? Losing a job, whether paid or volunteer? Having another baby? Taking care of an aging parent? Watching someone you love make bad life choices? Being parted from someone you love through death or divorce? We are usually unprepared for how difficult these times are. Each major transition requires an adjustment time from six months to two years. It's no wonder we get overwhelmed. At times I feel like yelling at the world; "Please keep still for five minutes so I can get used to the new state of things!"

For the really difficult possessions, the best time to deal with them is after we've built a firm foundation of organizational skills. Rather than start with things that we don't know what to do with, let's begin our home and life organization by learning on other people's stuff.

By beginning with our children's possessions, we can practice while being less emotionally involved. There will be some sentimental items, but remember, now they are older, messy people who need our help. As we take care of the house contents, we also need to train our children to take care of their own belongings and help with tasks that will benefit the whole family. If you don't have children, reading chapters related to children will still be worthwhile as the principles and strategies will apply elsewhere.

priorities

This concept revolutionized my thinking: every item we own should be aligned to our priorities in life. Most of us will have some decorative items and keepsakes, however, the majority of our belongings should serve a purpose. Whether we realize it or not, we live according to our priorities. Some priorities are necessities; others are passions. Below I've listed my current priorities along with related possessions.

1. Relationship with God — Bible, books, journal, music

2. Family & Friends — home and furnishings, car

3. Use my gifts & talents — computer, business resources, journal, art supplies
4. Self Care — bike, kayak, hiking gear, clothing

What are your priorities? Which are you passionate about? I am most passionate about my faith, relationships, and creative pursuits. Next, have a discussion with your husband and children to find out their priorities and passions. You may be surprised by their answers.

My husband and I both place a high priority on family time, as well as maintaining and building relationship with our kids, even as adults. At times we have a 'check-up' to see how things are going. My husband appreciates it when I let him know he needs to up the ante with relationships, at which time he adjusts the time he's away at work. We would rather have less income in exchange for good relationships.

As you consider and commit to the goal of organizing your whole home in line with your priorities, don't be discouraged. Work at your own pace, but remember to maintain the work that you've accomplished. Some people complete their homes over the course of a year. It may take that long if you've lived in one place for many years and have never purged and reorganized.

Some of us have purged occasionally and should be able to accomplish work rapidly. Ideally, get started and don't stop until you are finished. Take breaks for necessary things in life, which may include a job, appointments, and taking care of your family. Set your pace, but don't procrastinate or give up. You can do this! We can do this together. I'll guide you through your home, through rooms and categories, and we'll tackle the hard stuff later. If you have invited friends to join you, wait until everyone has a book and if needed, an additional blank journal. In the meantime, start purging your home.

heart check

God's word calls us to Love the Lord our God with all our heart, soul, mind, and strength. And to love others the same as we love ourselves. When I get into a mess, I wonder how I so easily strayed from those most important of priorities. I think, what am I running after? Fame? Fortune? Approval? Comfort? Or am I trying to prove to myself that I'm good enough and God will accept me if I accomplish something big for Him?

Lord,
Thank You that You love me and care about every detail of my life. Forgive me for thoughts, words, and actions that have led me away from You. Help me to walk in Your ways. Please grant me Your strength for this journey. I am excited that You reward those who diligently seek You.
Amen

resources & actions

You

- What are your Priorities and Related Possessions? Create a list in your Journal.

Family

- What are your Family Priorities? What are you husband's? Do some overlap with your own?

Group

- Read Mathew 11:28-30. Discuss the kind of lifestyle God can help us achieve. How will getting organized help?
- Share specific struggles and pray for each other, keeping all information strictly confidential.

journal

journal

3.

Children's and Teens' Rooms

clothing

Plan a time to go through your child's clothing with him. Remove all the clothing from the closet, drawers, and bring all the rest of his clothing from other parts of the house.

Have him try things on if there are items which he is not sure about. Let him decide what he'd like to keep. Don't force him to keep things you chose for him. Children grow fast anyway, so you'll only be delaying giving the items away.

As you are sorting, form five piles:

Give Away - Items you know you can pass to family, friends, or a charity which are in good condition.

Sell - Specialty items which were expensive to buy, and for which you know there is a market, such as hockey equipment, dance wear, elaborate costumes, school uniforms, etc.

Toss - Recycle whenever possible. Do not give your children's junky clothing to a thrift store. By doing so, you are giving them the task of paying to have it hauled to the landfill.

Repurpose - Is there a way to repurpose items? Some hand-knitted sweaters may be made into pillows. Try to limit these to just a few pieces, and place them in a Project Box.

Keepsakes - Limit these items to just a few. Otherwise, this collection will become too large. We'll look at some possibilities for keepsakes later.

In some cases, children won't select a wardrobe that covers all the bases. They may not want to keep essentials, such as a winter hat or underwear. (One child I know, did not wear underwear regularly until he was school-aged.) As the parent, you should say those items must be kept for now however, aim to reduce the volume to what will actually be used.

store clothing

If you have younger children or hope to have more babies, you need to sort and store outgrown clothing. It's best to store by size in boxes off the basement floor to ensure they don't get wet and moldy. Cardboard boxes work fine only if they are up higher than any potential flood should your water heater burst, or you experience another similar flooding disaster. Otherwise, use plastic containers. Simply mark the size/s on the outside of the box. Another option is to use plastic bins and place cardboard dividers inside, keeping sizes separate. Only keep clothing of good quality in good condition.

Short on space? Sometimes there are many years between siblings. We experienced a large gap between our second and third sons. There was no way I could store eight years' worth of clothing. I decided to give away useable clothing from our older boy. God provided everything we needed when we had to buy items for our younger son. I believe when we give away, we will always receive back what we need. God provides.

too large clothing

Some people buy clothing in larger sizes on sale, hoping the seasons will match up to their child's growth. I discourage clients from going beyond one or two sizes, since storage becomes an issue. Stores regularly have sales and second-hand clothing is plentiful.

arrange clothing in the closet

Arrange clothing to make it all visible. Do not rotate seasonal clothing. However, winter coats are most logically kept in a closet or on a hook by the front door during the cold season and tucked into the bedroom closet for summer. Most homes have plenty of storage with existing closets or with a purchased wardrobe and one additional dresser per child. Even a small dresser with a small closet will do just fine. If storage is a problem, your child has too much and you need to continue paring down until it all fits into the available space.

Put all the wearable clothing inside the closet, beginning with the heavy coats on the end that is partially blocked by closet doors; otherwise, left to right works well. The lineup for girls: coats, jackets, sweaters, pants, dresses, skirts, tops.

The order of colour doesn't actually matter. Primarily focus on grouping like items. However, if you enjoy the process, try sorting by colour as well. Put the darkest colours toward the same side as the heavy coats, then layer in the other colors: black, navy blue, brown, red, purple, green, orange, fuchsia, lavender, pink, cream, white.

Place patterned clothing with the most dominate colour, or place all your pattered clothing in one section. Another section may be plaids or stripes, if you have enough garments to warrant doing so. Any specialty clothing, such as dance wear, may have its own section.

Once you have clothing assembled on the closet rods by type and colour, within each section arrange the clothing heavyweight to lightweight. For example, within the Tops section, first long sleeved dark tops to long sleeved light tops; next come the short sleeved tops by colour and fabric weight, followed by sleeveless and tank tops. Some girls prefer to keep their tank tops in a dresser drawer.

Some clients prefer dress pants, jeans, and sport pants to be hung; personally, I prefer to fold all pants and place them on the closet shelf or in drawers.

how much clothing and footwear?

Clients always ask how much clothing they should keep for their children. People with a lot of clothing find it isn't all worn. And if they don't do laundry regularly, the laundry pile grows to gargantuan proportions. One pile I saw took up the entire laundry room floor space, half way up the appliances. I think a good amount of clothing is two week's worth. That is not counting coats or formal wear. A full set with layers for one solid seven day week in the summer, and another solid week's worth for the winter. Most items may be worn all year when layered. Jackets and sweaters are utilized on cool summer nights.

To mentally prepare, imagine packing for a two-week holiday: one week in the summer, and one week in the winter. When I go on a trip, I pack my favourite clothing. I recommend clients keep clothing they enjoy wearing, which they wear regularly already, and is in good condition.

For those of us who live in the north with extreme temperatures on both end of the thermostat, it is reasonable to have two sets of outer clothing for children, snow pants and sporty coat for play, as well as a dressy winter coat for going to the theatre, the movies, to parties, and church. Waterproof splash pants are also essential for spring and fall play.

As for boots, given the length of the cold season in some areas, two to four pairs of winter boots of various types are acceptable, as long as they are worn regularly. Seasonal footwear may include a pair of rain boots, gym shoes, dress shoes, and snow boots. In the summer, children need a sturdy pair of walking sandals, water shoes, and flip flops.

Fortunately, footwear and clothing are relatively inexpensive for young children, and little ones do not wear out their clothing or shoes making second hand websites and stores a goldmine for thrifty parents.

Consider your family's unique circumstances. In my family, we go barefoot a lot around the house and yard in the summer. I think it's good for us and saves on shoes. In the area where we live, I found water shoes for swimming were important because of all the rocks, mud, and sharp bits at shorelines and water parks. Use your own discretion.

dressers & shelves

Have containers ready for items being tossed, donated, or being returned to elsewhere in the house. First have your daughter make her bed, then empty out all the drawers onto the bed.

Dresser drawers are the perfect place for small and personal items: underwear, socks, nightwear, swimsuits, shorts, and sport pants, for those storing pants in drawers. Older girls will need either a drawer or container for their tank tops as many fashions require layering. Clothing should be either rolled or folded small so that all the items in the drawers are visible all at once.

One of my teen clients did not like to fold her clothing, but she enjoyed rolling her tops and stacking the sausage shapes in the sections of a closet organizer her parents had installed. First she'd fold in the sides, leaving one third in the middle, then she rolled from the top down.

Teen girls may also like to have drawers in a bedside table or desk for makeup, crafts, sewing, their favorite sport or hobby, and jewelry. As a general rule, small items require small containers and every single item must be sorted with like items. You could help her choose inexpensive plastic or cardboard boxes or containers at a Dollar Store, IKEA, craft store, or repurpose boxes from the pantry by covering them with fabric or sticky shelf paper.

If she likes to keep her own book collection, make sure she has a bookshelf in her room. Rather than buying more and larger book shelves, limit her to one or two sets which could also display a few mementos along the top.

When tables, desks, and shelves are empty, re-imagine the spaces. Allow your son to decide what he would like to keep in his room and what he'd like to discard. Don't use guilt. He shouldn't have to keep any gifts or items passed on to him if he truly can't use them or doesn't enjoy them.

By allowing him to decide how he'd like to organize his room, he's training for the future. As he is given leadership over his own space, he will be much more likely to care for his space. In fact, make sure he understands that after this redo, he is responsible to keep everything picked up, surfaces and display items dusted, and everything in their homes. Every item needs a home, which is the cardinal rule of organizing.

When sorting items by type, look for one group first to make it less overwhelming. For example, look for all the stuffed toys, put them in a pile, let your son decide which ones will go to new homes. Let him know another child is excited to have a new stuffed pet to love.

Once all the items are sorted into groups, decide where "home" will be for each group. They may be in boxes or containers in the closet, on the shelves, or in containers on the floor. Stuffed toys work well in a toy hammock suspended from a corner, or repurpose a shoe sorter on the back of a door.

It is best with young children not to have sets accessible so they don't empty all the containers at once. Try to put small, difficult to clean up sets like puzzles and tiny toys up on the highest shelves if you must store them in the child's bedroom.

As for books, bedtime stories are wonderful and it is a quiet activity for children which helps them unwind and get ready to sleep. A small collection of books near the bed is great, but once it overflows, the excess books will need a place on a family bookshelf in another room.

Bedrooms are for resting. Some things which should never be kept in a child's room are a TV or computer. Also causing an unrestful place are too many toys, too many collectables, and too many books. Bedrooms are for resting. Sometimes, children enjoy using their bedrooms for playing if they have a Lego table with their own collection of blocks, or a Playmobil setup which they'd like to keep from younger siblings. But generally, it's best to keep bedrooms clear, uncluttered, and restful so the child can sleep well.

If at all possible, it is best to have a playroom in a different part of the house, as well as a computer centre which is in an open place where parents walk by frequently.

For older teens and young adults, especially if they have younger siblings, they should have their personal items in their rooms, including all the items they bring in to the house after they've been out all day to school or work.

wall art

The general rule for wall art including bulletin boards is that they are to be put up with help from a parent so they are level and secure. Once they're up, bulletin boards are a fun place to display just about anything from school art, postcards, photos, badges, stickers, travel pins, buttons. For younger children, you can make or buy a bulletin board with ribbon for holding items, but for older children, about age five and up, you may use push-pins as long as you have a safety talk with them beforehand. If they break the rules, stand firm and remove the board and push pins until the child is older and can safely use them.

Personally, I like simple, clean art and displays which allows a bedroom to be easy on the eyes and restful to the soul. If a child asks to put up a poster, you certainly have the right to say no. We don't do posters in our house. But consider that he is learning to decorate and take care of his own space. It is good to have some rules as to what you allow on the walls. Decide ahead of time where you'll draw the line.

You may never have a child who pushes the limits, but there is sometimes a child in the family who is a unique gift; a Humbler. God sends them to us so we can realize we are not perfect, and we do not have the perfect recipe for being a parent. That wonderful, creative, push-the-limits child will be an amazing leader one day, but he or she needs to be mentored in a consistent, loving way. So, if you have a Humbler, remember that it's an opportunity for personal growth for you both.

heart check

Sometimes it is difficult to remember that children are a gift from God, especially when they make big messes. And have I seen big messes. I grew up in an old country home on a small acreage near Stoney Creek, Ontario. We were not far from the big city of Hamilton, not far from the shores of Lake Ontario, and not far from Niagara Falls. There were six of us and we were often sent outside to play for the day. We went down to a creek and played on the rocks and in the water. We climbed trees, made mud pies at the bank of a small pond among bulrushes, and had fun throwing them at each other and the house.

I know I wasn't a dream child yet it was easy to keep track of my few special items, such as a doll, art supplies, and my favorite books and notebooks for writing. Even after I was married, our place was fine. It wasn't until my husband and I started a family that I discovered my limitations. Toys littered the floor from one end of the house to the other. Laundry multiplied, dishes piled up, and I liked reading better than housework.

Fortunately, as a young mum, I had some wonderful older ladies who encouraged me to be a good mom and wife without saying anything, showing me how to keep an organized home. It was a struggle, but things got easier as I trained my children to help. Later we'll look at age appropriate tasks for children.

Lord,
Thank You that my children are a gift from You. Help me to appreciate them, love them, care for them, but also gain the skills I need to train them to help.
Please be with me on the journey. Help me to get unstuck and be diligent to take care of what You've already given to me.
Amen.

resources & actions

You

- Read, *Hold On to Your Kids: Why Parents Need to Matter More Than Peers,* Gordon Neufeld, Gabor Mate M.D.

- If you are married, ask your spouse to read it, too.
- Journal a prayer for each of your children in the journal section below, or use a separate journal.

Family

- Have a family garage sale and together decide on a reward.
- Begin a family tidy time each day, for ten minutes. Put on the timer and everyone race to see who is finished first. Do it every day and it will become habit.

Group

- Read Luke 6:46-49 with your group. Discuss the role intentionally building a firm foundation should have in your homes.
- Pray for each other.

journal

journal

4.

Kitchen

food

Kitchens are often referred to as the heart of the home. There we produce nutritious meals and baked goods, nourishing bodies and souls of our loved ones. I don't know about you, but when I'm stressed and going through a difficult transition, I sometimes stop cooking. Or I'll cook easy, not very nutritious meals. Whatever is going on in my life will inevitably seem worse because my body becomes run down and lethargic, feeding my thought life with negativity. And without good food and proper exercise, I don't sleep well. It becomes a downhill spiral that takes focused energy to overcome.

In the kitchen start by emptying the fridge. Toss expired food and any garbage food which makes you feel worse when you eat it. Fresh meat lasts only a day before it needs to be cooked. Cooked food expires in one week.

Next, take out the shelves and drawers and wash them at the sink with hot, soapy water. Rinse and let shelves and racks air dry on the counter, on top of tea towels. While they dry, wipe out the entire fridge. Repeat the process with the freezer. Toss any items that are old as they have lost their nutritional value.

freezer foods storage guide

6 to 9 months: beef, lamb, pork, veal

6 to 7 months: nuts, dried fruit, jellies and jams

6 months: cheese

3 to 6 months: pasteurized cream

3 to 4 months: sausages and organ meats

2 to 3 months: ground meat (chicken, turkey, beef, lamb, etc.)

3 months: meat loaf and other prepared meats, as seasonings deteriorate

3 to 4 months: fish and seafood

2 to 3 months: poultry

3 months: butter

2 months: unbaked cookies and biscuits

1 month: pasteurized milk

1 week: uncooked bread dough

If you have a deepfreeze, empty it and wash it thoroughly with a mild cleanser. Double-bag the wasted food in large garbage bags and if you can't fit it all in to your curb-side garbage can, plan to take a drive to the landfill as soon as possible.

The fridge and freezer will dry fairly quickly. If there are stains or odors, use baking soda as an abrasive, or a safe cleaner to tackle them. You may leave an open box of baking soda inside the fridge and freezer to absorb odors.

When you put the food back inside, group like items together to create a system to help you find things quickly. Date items when adding to the freezers and place the oldest items on top or front to use first.

From this day forward, promise yourself you will try harder to eat healthy, wholesome foods, and provide them as much as possible for your family. Their health depends a lot on what we feed them. I've included suggested resources below to help on this quest.

cooking supplies

Before tackling the cookware, start the oven on its self-clean cycle, or spray it with oven cleaner to do its work while you sort the kitchen.

We often begin our married lives with inexpensive and/or mismatched cookware. Somewhere along the line, or as wedding gifts, every couple needs a good quality set of cooking pots, two or three frying pans, one or two roasting pans, plus utensils.

Most pot sets do not come with all the pots you will need. I like to have a large steamer which doubles as a heavy-duty sieve. Also, I need a large stock pot which I use for making double-batch meals or soups when cooking for a crowd.

Remove the pots and pans from their cupboard and make some hard decisions about what you really use. Instead of relegating all the oldies to a camping box or overstuffing your trailer, give them to a thrift store where another person just getting started in their first home will put them to use.

When you return pots to the cupboards, make sure you put large ones at the back and small ones at the front so you can see everything. Stack them if space is limited and try to put all the lids either in a holder fastened to the cupboard door, or in a separate drawer. Another tactic is to nestle lids inside matching pots.

Are you emotionally attached to your pots? It can be a problem parting with them if you remember when you met your sweetheart and he cooked pasta for you from the old enamel aluminum pot with the wheat picture on the front. Is there a way to capture the moment so you can give the pot away and move on?

You could take a snapshot of it. After the day's work, sit down with your journal, list the items you found difficult to part with, and write a few sentences about the memories associated with the items. It will be a sweet remembrance for you to share with your sweetheart at a future dinner, using your new, better quality pots. Cook him the same simple but delicious meal, and thank him for the great memory. You'll be using the old item and memory as a jumping off point to create a new memory. Don't live in the past, but use the past to springboard into the future and continue living in the present and loving those who are with you.

If he isn't any longer with you because divorce or death parted you, allow the pain to come, look at it, feel it for a few minutes, and then remember how you are feeling stronger and more settled every day. Remember to breathe deeply. Moving on with your life doesn't mean you didn't love the person, but you are acknowledging that they have moved on, whether by God's choice or theirs, and it is time for you to move on, too. Again, it may be appropriate to snap a photo and journal about your feelings later, after you've finished the room you are working on. Keep going; you're almost through the kitchen!

utensils

Many people can't find a flipper when they need one. Empty all the utensil drawers and holders if you have one or more on the counter, and spread them out to see what you've acquired. Add to your "give" bin the ones you don't use anymore. If you are unsure, put all the utensils in a container in your pantry or another location. Whenever you need a utensil, go and get the right one. At the end of two weeks, see what's left in the bin. If you have limited space, you'll want to get rid of everything you haven't used. If space isn't a problem, by all means keep the grapefruit spoon, the melon-ball maker and the pastry edger. But will you use them ever? If you haven't used them in the past year, it's likely you never will. Go ahead and move the items into the Give box. You'll be glad you did.

I like to think about the times my family stayed in a vacation rental with a full kitchen, equipped with the basics. The funny thing is, I did not miss the things which clutter up my kitchen cupboards and drawers. We somehow managed with one bowl, one plastic sieve, a small pot set, one frying pan, and one roaster. There would also be a small set of cooking utensils and maybe two or three knives. Vacation rentals are so restful because they are sparse.

Aim to reduce utensils, as well as other tools and equipment, until your space is uncluttered. An uncluttered workspace will promote a calm atmosphere: it will be easy to find and use items when you need them.

knives

Knives are one kitchen implement where you shouldn't scrimp. Invest in at least two top quality knives: a paring knife and a medium sized knife good for slicing and chopping. If they aren't in the budget, ask for them as gifts from family when holidays roll around.

For storing, there are some reasonably priced knife holders available that fit inside a drawer. Others prefer a knife block on the counter. I'd rather have them hidden to keep my counters clear.

dishes

When my husband and I were newlyweds, we bought one set of dishes. They served us just fine. As time went by and we were invited to friends' homes for meals, I noticed that some women had two or more additional sets of dishes. It seemed like a wonderful idea to invest in several sets and set the table appropriately for various holidays and events. In hindsight, that was a mistaken notion. I bought a second set which no one liked much or used. The whole family gravitates to the one, plain white, basic dish set I've had our entire married lives. I have replenished them, as I like to have four sets all at once. They serve about 12 to 16 people easily.

With white dishes, we can change placemats, the table cloth, candles, and napkins for a different look each time. Basic white is the only color anyone ever needs.

small appliances

Your kitchen shouldn't look like Home Hardware's Small Appliance department. You don't need to own every device ever invented by man. Admit it: most of them you've used once or twice, then the novelty wore off. To justify space in the kitchen, an appliance must be used regularly and make life easier. If you are just as quick slicing carrots for soup with a knife and cutting board as using a slicer that has to be disassembled and cleaned, why bother with it?

There are several essentials in my home: coffeemaker, kettle, toaster, crock pot, large griddle (which will cook a large volume), a good quality blender (for smoothies), a food processor. Some people absolutely love their toaster ovens, but I've never had one and get by fine with my oven broiler. Every other gadget we've had, from ice cream makers (too small) and rice cookers (hard to clean), we don't miss one bit.

spices

Spices should be kept so you can see them all. The worse place to keep them is on the back of your stove where steam, heat, grease, and light destroy their quality. It's best to keep them in a shallow cupboard or drawer. Lie them down in a drawer with all the labels facing up, or buy an insert to make them visible and accessible.

Cupboard and drawer accessories are easy to find and inexpensive at places such as Amazon online. Secure opened bags of spices with clamps. Group small packages in small open top containers, even if you have to pull them out to look down inside them. At least they will be in a group of like spices and you'll see them all at once and probably use many of them together. You could have an Italian Food spice container; an Indian Meal spice holder, etc.

Many people purchase sets of matching bottles or containers with plans to create a beautiful spice display in a handy place close to the stove. Please don't buy these if you haven't already. One hundred percent of people I've met with matching sets of bottles never use them. If you have a lot of extra time and you disagree with me, insisting you would use them, you should easily be able to find a set second-hand.

Baking supplies can also be kept in their original packages if you secure them tightly and place them in a larger container which is plastic, glass or metal. It's best not to use cardboard to hold food packages, since it could wet through from oil and cause mold or other problems. Liquids such as food coloring, flavorings such as vanilla, orange, and almond should definitely be stored inside a spill-proof container to prevent cupboard damage.

arranging cupboards

If you have deep cupboards, use long, narrow containers or racks which you pull forward to access the contents. If your budget allows, shop for cupboard inserts such as wire racks, shelves, and turntables which are easily installed.

Most kitchen designs are logical and it's self-evident: cooking pots and pans near the stove and oven; coffee cups near the coffee maker; utensils in the drawer near the dish-cupboard and both utensils and plates near the table. If you declutter and eliminate unneeded and expired items, there should be enough space to store the rest. If you truly have an inadequate kitchen, consider utilizing a nearby closet as a pantry.

In large families, it works well for each person to have their own coffee/tea cup. That way it's obvious who left their cup out on the table. One family with six children gave each child their own colour for cups, dishes, toothbrushes, towels, and even their socks and underwear. I thought it was a clever idea.

decorations

Kitchens tend to catch a myriad of decorative items: everything from fridge magnets and window sun-catchers to souvenirs and spoon collections. These types of items are dust and grease catchers. Try to eliminate visual clutter. The worst thing to do with unwanted items is to force them on someone else. Either sell them, give them away to charity, return gifts to the giver, or use them.

heart check

When taking care of my family and myself, I want to purchase just enough food for our use, without having to toss out items that have gone bad. With adult kids moving out and coming back, plus unexpected dinner guests at times, it's challenging to adjust our cooking to match. I want our lives around food to be frugal.

I also feel challenged to eat healthy, unprocessed foods, as close as possible to how God created them: whole grains, lots of vegetables and fruit, legumes, nuts, and seeds. Research shows our society eats too much meat. Additionally, cow milk was designed to be wonderful for baby cows, but not so much for people. As I have educated myself about whole foods and work to gradually adjust my family's menu, I've been surprised by the level of resistance—from myself and others. We have focused on food as so much more than simply fuel for our bodies.

Food has become what feeds our desire for good taste, for entertainment, for filling up our hearts when we are sad, lonely, or bored. We also have a teen who will battle over food choices as he exerts his growing independence. My husband and I very much need God's grace and His wisdom to help us be good examples. It is a battle, yet God cares and is interested in every area of our lives.

Do we follow fad diets, and buy expensive drinks and supplements? How often, if ever, do we fast and pray? Do we go to God with empty stomachs, hungry for Him in our lives?

Father God,
Thank You for the abundance You have given to us.
Bless our food. I ask that You help us plan healthy
meals and snacks, shopping within our family

budget, avoiding waste. And where we are struggling to honour You with our eating and with our fasting, we ask for Your grace and wisdom, which You give to all who ask without finding fault. We are needy and hungry for You, God. Fill us with Your Spirit.
Amen.

resources & actions

You

- Use cookbooks or online recipe sites, to plan family meals for two weeks, making sure everyone picks at least one favourite meal per week.
- Make a shopping list to match your meal plan.
- Journal to explore your relationship with food.

Family

- Watch movies, *Forks Over Knives, Food Inc., and Hungry For Change.* By researching many views, discuss what could be a balanced view.
- Give to a food bank.

- Sponsor a child through Feed The Hungry or Compassion.
- Make a meal for a youth group, at a Soup Kitchen, or for a family dealing with illness.
- Consider doing a fast. Research The Daniel Fast, or consider substituting one meal a day or week with just vegetable juice while you pray.

Group

- Read 1 Corinthians 10:31. What does it mean, to do all to the glory of God?
- Read Matthew 7:7-12 and Mathew 14:13-21. Discuss the example Jesus set for us. How did Jesus respond to demands put on Him?
- Pray for each other.

journal

journal

5.

The Dining Room

Sit with your favorite beverage in a location where you can see several main rooms in your home and think about the use of space. How are the spaces used? Is there an activity that needs a dedicated space? Often the home dictates how rooms are used and it works, as in the case of the kitchen with various cupboards for things near the fridge and stove. But the dining room may be a spare room of sorts; a flex room that will better serve as an office, a guest room, a craft or sewing room, a homeschooling room, a library, a painting studio, a den, a workstation, or whatever is needed.

If you do intend to repurpose the dining room, try to find appropriate shelves, desks, tables, cabinets and whatever else you will need to be properly equipped. Look for second hand items over new to keep more items out of landfills. Buy or make compartments for your organizational needs.

If however, your dining room is actually going to be used for dining and entertaining, aim for a cheerful space, uncluttered, with art on the walls and seasonal decorations. Empty cabinets and clean them. Make sure you only keep items you use or truly love. Sell, give away, or recycle the rest; resist the urge to move items into your newly cleared out and organized kitchen.

A general rule is to have a table large enough to accommodate your immediate family, plus two. Then if you have over a child's closest friends for a family birthday dinner, it will be easy to fit them in. If your budget allows, buy a table with one or two leaves for expansion. Having two extra matching chairs tucked into corners of the dining or living room work well, but if cost or space is an issue, try buying a couple of folding chairs. Better yet, buy or make cubes, step stools, or ottomans which can double as seating or tables in other rooms when not in use.

Maybe it sounds silly, but lighting and sunlight are concerns in the dining room. We've had people over and they sit where the setting summer sun scorches their retinas. They are too polite to say anything and insist it's fine, but without asking, if you notice the sun is an issue, just pull the shade down, close the curtains, or steal their chair when they get up and insist they take yours.

Another lighting issue is fixtures. Our overhead light which holds eight bulbs is way too bright for a relaxing dinner, but would work well for open heart surgery. To remediate the problem, I've put a large table lamp on a long, narrow table in front of a window in the dining nook, which we use during dinner. It is bright enough in combination with light coming from adjoining rooms.

If you don't have a dimmer switch and can't install one, consider the light sources and make everyone's dining experience calm and enjoyable however possible.

china

Many women receive china when they marry. I am thankful I only have a china tea set passed down to us from my mother-in-law. We have used it a fair bit, for fun tea parties, birthday teas, and more recently when my teen son wanted to remember how special those times were.

Most mothers give those sorts of things to their eldest daughter, but I am thinking our youngest son's wife would feel special if she received it, since I married the youngest son of a family.

There may be matching dishes somewhere, but truthfully I would rather the person who has them enjoy them, as they would likely be a burden to me. There's no point in being bitter about such things; instead I treasure and occasionally enjoy using the tea set and display it in a glass-front cupboard in my kitchen.

People are realizing now that it is pointless to have a cabinet full of expensive dishes they rarely if ever use. If you have china, use it. If you don't like your china and never use it, turn it into a gift or sell it. Remember, we own our stuff; our stuff shouldn't own us.

serving dishes

With serving dishes, consider the largest group you have and will again entertain. Hosting usually requires having several large platters, large bowls, and dessert dishes. An alternative is to buy disposable serving dishes for the holidays then donate them to the thrift store, since most people don't have large gatherings every year.

My most used serving dishes double as glass baking pans, baking bowls, and dinner plates.

I do have an inexpensive soup tureen and two gravy boats work best. I make soup often and I enjoy putting the tureen on the dining table; and when we have a large family dinner during the holidays, two gravy boats make things easier. Every item must meet two criteria: is it useful, and is there space to store it?

heart check

All of us should invite people over and offer friendship, whether often or occasionally. It is difficult to move in to a new town or city away from family and being invited over is a real treat. As a young mum, new at church, I felt loved by an older lady who invited me over for canned soup and tuna sandwiches. She didn't prepare a fancy meal, but the gesture filled my heart with joy. She was demonstrating God's love to me as I had talked with God just that morning about how lonely I felt leaving the work world to become a work-at-home mother. When we pray and ask God, often He will bring someone to mind who could use a friend.

It is with a sad heart that I have to admit there have been some uncomfortable dinners at my table. Sometimes we think we need to continue to have people in our lives no matter what they do. That is not so. It is okay to have boundaries, at least for a time, to protect our family and ourselves. Doing so may be a part of mental and spiritual health for us. If that is your experience too, don't forget to pray for them.

My Father in Heaven,
I dedicate my home to You. May it be a place where Your name is honored. Fill our hearts with gratitude for all You have provided. Bless our table and our gatherings. May we encourage others. Give us wisdom to help those who are struggling around us. Amen.

resources & actions

You

- Read Psalm 34 and mediate on it.
- Read *Boundaries*, Henry Cloud, 2002
- Find your personality type at www.16personalities.com or use a similar Myers-Briggs indicator quiz. I believe personality types are generalizations about tribes God created, yet within each tribe each person is unique.
- Get feedback from those close to you, and decide if your result is accurate.
- Add discoveries, thoughts and feelings to your journal.

Family

- Pray for relatives and friends who are struggling.

Group

- Exchange findings about personality types.

- Read Galatians 5:22-23. Which fruit do you struggle with?
- Read John 15:1-17 and discuss. What are the results of remaining in Jesus?
- Pray for each other.

journal

journal

6.

Pantry & Other Storage

pantry

There are many different types and sizes of pantries. Most modern pantries are the size of a small closet with shelves from floor to ceiling. Ideally, all the shallow shelves have items on them which are visible. This helps when you meal plan and scour the pantry to see what you already have, so you don't buy duplicates.

Purge and reorganize: empty the entire pantry. Toss expired food.

pantry food storage

5 years: commercially dehydrated foods, if packaged properly

2 years: salt, sugar, whole peppercorns, dried spices stored in a cool, dark place

18 months: canned meat, poultry and veggies (except for sauerkraut and tomatoes alone or in other products); canned fruit (except citrus, juices, and berries); dried legumes stored in stainless steel or aluminum containers

12 to 18 months: professionally freeze-dried foods

1 year: canned fish, hydrogenated fats and oils, flour, boxed cereal in original containers, canned nuts, instant pudding, instant dry cream and bouillon products, soda and baking powder, dried herbs stored in a cool, dark place

6 months: evaporated milk, nonfat dry whole milk in metal containers, condensed meat and beef soups, dried fruit in metal containers, canned citrus fruit, juices, canned berries

The taste and nutritional quality of food deteriorates over time, so it is best to not keep a large stockpile. Some people like to keep a year's worth of food. I believe this is out of fear of a disaster, and they want to be prepared. Do not base your life on fear, but rather on reality. It is wise to keep at least two weeks' worth of food in the house in case of a storm, illness, or power outage. Beyond that, stores and warehouses around the country will have provisions.

If you really want to prepare for anything, teach your kids how to find food in the wilderness near your home. There are some great wilderness survival guides available. You just never know when there'll be a zombie apocalypse (joking).

In my family, we taught our children to pick berries and how to keep a small garden, and most of us know how to fish and hunt. Those are skills that can be learned and passed down. They are life skills everyone should know.

In recent years, there has been additional evidence that flours and oils do not keep well. With so many foods losing their nutritional value with storage, it is best to shop for fresh food at least once a week.

other storage

For those of us with extra large pantries, we have the added challenge of not using them as a general dumping ground. I have decided to use my large pantry for all the household storage, except for sporting goods and tools which belong in the garage.

Most will likely need a storage area in a different part of the house, such as under stairs, a utility room in the basement, under a high deck or porch, or in a closet. I'm convinced there is a law of attraction in empty places which draws stuff to it. It's time to decrease the amount of things we store. What are we storing things for? We don't usually use those things any more. And keepsakes, which we'll talk about later, are not appreciated if they are tucked away in boxes in a dark basement, under the stairs, or in an attic.

Begin by emptying your storage area and get rid of everything possible. If there are things your husband or children are storing, you do need to ask them first, but the easy answer for them is to keep everything. That is really not a good reply because you know it isn't working. You feel stuck; the house is crammed with things no one needs; you need to clean things out and get a fresh start.

Encourage them to let go of belongings, but don't force as relationships are more important.

One of the items my husband wouldn't let me give away or sell for years is an older pressure canner about the size of a small child. I stored it for a decade, but I kept asking him about it each year when I tidied the basement storage area. He was attached to it because his parents had used it to can salmon. His heart strings wouldn't allow him to part with it. Finally, we talked about how we would never use it. We hadn't used it in ten years and we were highly unlikely to use it in the future. We like to fish, but we like to eat fresh fish, instead of taking the time to can our catch. He relented, and we found a good home for it with friends who do a lot of canning. It turned into a great gift. It makes me happy thinking about the young family using it. My husband is happy about it, too.

Following are several categories which may be stored in the pantry or other storage area.

linens

I keep two baskets on a shelf to serve as my main floor linen closet. In one I keep kitchen towels, dish cloths, and pot holders. In the other I keep table linens such as placemats and table cloths. Because table linens are an easy, compact way to change the entire look of a room, I keep two sets of cloth placemats, in yellow and red, a set of sturdy floral cork placemats, and four table cloths.

I have one spring table cloth in a bright floral, a purple one, burgundy holiday cloth, and a plaid one which works well in the autumn. The cloth linens are all rolled up and stand up in one of the baskets. By storing them this way, I can see at a glance what I need. I recently added a laundry basket, just a small one on a bottom shelf, for the soiled kitchen and table linens.

gift wrap

One clear, long container for any occasion, and one for Christmas. Some clients prefer a standing gift wrap storage container. These may also be stored under a bed if space is limited.

sewing supplies

Divided containers house threads, small sewing supplies, plus a larger clear bin for fabrics. It's a good idea to regularly purge unused fabric. A quilter will appreciate any gifts of cotton. Polyester fabrics may be recycled.

electronics

Cords and chargers in a container. It is a good idea to label cords with tape as soon as you bring them in the house. Then you'll never have the problem of figuring out which cord goes with which device.

toys

As discussed in other sections, toys should be stored in containers. Toys for visiting children may be kept in a storage area.

small appliances

Group them together in one section. Do not keep boxes as they add bulk and people generally don't reuse them.

pantry food

Some clients like transferring dry goods to plastic storage containers. In theory it sounds like a good idea, but often food is stored too long and goes rancid. For many it's an unwanted extra step. Most people have good intentions for those containers but don't follow through. I suggest you forego them to save time.

Rotate food as grocery stores do: put oldest at front to use first. Group like products. Place large, light containers on the top shelf, and heavy large containers on lower shelves.

office

If your home lacks a main floor office or desk, a small section of the pantry may serve as an office. Keep smaller items grouped together in baskets or containers.

seasonal decorations

Large, clear plastic bins with snap down lids work well. Limit decorations to one bin for each season, depending on your space limitations. Less is better.

recycling

I keep small recycling bins in the pantry for paper and food packaging. I pop things in there while I'm working then take the full bins out to our large recycling bins.

garage

There are all sorts of products available to organize the garage. The simplest are open shelves; more complicated systems are available through garage experts. Hooks from the ceiling provide additional storage for bikes, kayaks, and other items. All objects should be grouped together and stored in appropriately sized containers with lids, to keep out dust. Paints, cleaners, and other toxic products should be stored on upper shelves away from children and pets. Watch for your community's toxic round-up or take to a recycling centre.

Everything needs a home and everyone in the family needs to know where things go. Once you declutter and reorganize, give your family a guided tour to explain the new system to them; otherwise you'll find things in the wrong places.

Your pantry and other storage areas should only have things you use. After a year or so, empty your pantry and storage areas again and see what needs to go. Items which your family resisted parting with will have much weaker arguments for staying. Each year, as you continue to refine your systems, you will gain momentum. Don't just maintain; aim to improve each year. As you do, it will get easier, the family will be more cooperative, and life will be less complicated and overwhelming.

heart check

What are you storing? I promised to leave the hard stuff for the end, so if you are storing things of this category, you have my permission to take them, box them up if you haven't already, and put them in a place where you can deal with them later. Usually these fall into the Keepsakes and Photos categories. Remember that letting go of the past may be difficult but necessary to moving ahead into the future God has for you.

Often when we go through a difficult time it is because the problem is within ourselves, not other people. No one can make us feel or react a certain way. Personally, I don't want to recoil from life because of past painful experiences. When I get hurt, I take it to God. I ask Him to heal me. I ask Him to bind up my wounds. I pray for help to forgive others. I tell God I forgive them. I do all I can to get right with God and with others.

We may purge our physical belongings, but we must also purge our hearts from time to time, preferably daily. When we are clean-hearted, we can better operate within our tribe, displaying the fruit of the Spirit.

Sometimes I think about the grand movement of the earth and stars in the universe—like an orchestra synchronized by a loving Conductor. I want to know my part in it.

Father God,
I ask for diligence to keep going on this decluttering and reorganizing project. I ask for Your grace to carry me when I get discouraged or overwhelmed. Give me Your strength, Lord. And for the things I come across which tug at my heartstrings, or the heartstrings of my family, help me to be sensitive and kind, knowing that it will be easier to let go with time.
And Lord, help me to always forgive and get a bigger picture of what You're doing.
Amen.

resources & actions

You

- Read, *The Calvary Road*, Roy Hession.

- Check out *Real Simple Magazine.* www.realsimple.com.
- Has God put His finger on anything in your heart? Record it in your journal.

Family

- Read, *The Five Love Languages,* by Gary Chapman. What is each person's love language?

Group

- Read James 4:1-12. Discuss how conflicts happen within and outside one's self.
- Read Philippians 4:4-8. Discuss how to 'think about' things with positive attributes.
- Pray for each other.

journal

journal

7.

Entryways

The entryway is the first place where your home gives people a welcome hug. They are sanctuaries where we can rest in peaceful surroundings and be nourished with good food for our bodies, minds, and souls. Some view the home as a shadow of our future home in Heaven.

It needs to be neat for safety reasons, in case there is ever a fire or other emergency and everyone needs to get out fast.

rugs

Something of great importance at entryways is to have nonslip throw rugs to catch dirt; the longer the runner or rug, the better. These longer rugs do wonders to keep the floors clean. We've trained our dogs to come in at the back garden door and lie down on the rug there, until their paws are dry. Our floor stays surprisingly clean considering we have eight paws plus family and friends coming and going.

It is also worth investing in small rugs for just outside each entrance, made of natural fibers. They do get really dirty, but that just shows they are doing their job. If you buy inexpensive ones, you can either throw them into the washing machine, or hose them off outside. When they get really tattered, toss them out and buy new ones. Natural fibers are earth friendly and will decompose quickly.

closets & hooks

Hangers in closets take too much time and effort for most people. Hooks for a busy family, especially with young children, work much better. Install a row of hooks with a shelf above to make an attractive alternative to a closet where things get lost. If possible, it is best to have two hooks for each person plus at least one basket above for gloves and hats. Below, against the wall, add boot racks or drip trays on mats.

If you have room in your entryway, hall trees with hooks for coats and attached bench with drawers for storage are wonderful. Our children all use our hall tree hooks for their coats and hats over using the closet. As a result, I'll either ask them to move their jackets into the closet, or I'll do it periodically.

Shoes and boots can be a real problem, especially if you live in a location with varied weather. When there is a shortage of space, some families don't bother trying to make shoe and boot storage look fancy; they have simply opted for open shelf units close to their main entrance where family puts their footwear. Function must win over beauty. Another simple solution is hanging cloth shoe holders in a closet, to multiply storage.

drop zones

Every house has a spot where people like to drop their belongings when they return home. The kitchen island is ours. I ask people to remove their things, but if I'm tidying when they aren't around, I use their baskets as a catchall.

I keep another basket in the pantry for my incoming mail. I don't like clutter on my kitchen counters and I check my mail basket regularly. If mail needs attention or filing, I take it to my office desk and deal with it as soon as possible. When I open the mail, I drop the useless paper right into the recycle bin.

At my office desk, I put things that can wait into a paper sorter with items needing attention first at the front; the rest are put in order of when they are due. This system works remarkably well and I recommend it to all my clients. Most clients will keep a paper sorter on a desk or kitchen counter. It may also be installed on a wall.

heart check

Think about the climate you'd like to set in your home. We should keep out stress, busyness, harmful influences, and degrading words and actions. We want to let in family and friends, celebrations, new opportunities to learn and grow, and anything that will help us draw closer to God and each other.

Any time we feel a twinge of guilt or anxiety, we should ask God if we have offended Him or allowed something harmful into our homes and hearts. Sometimes we make mistakes, but God forgives, heals, and cleanses.

Other times, another person in our family has a bad attitude or brings something into the home to disturb the peace. Remember, the goal isn't to have a perfect show home at the expense of those living in the house. Instead, the goal is inner peace and close relationships. Our home and possessions are there to serve us. If you need to invest a lot of time with someone going through a difficult time, the house can wait. People always take priority. When things calm down, you'll be able to return to your organizing routine. Be determined to complete the project, but sensitive to your family.

Father God,
Be our Doorkeeper. Fill our home with Your peace;
cover it with Your protection. Forgive us for tracking
mud into our hearts and homes. Forgive us. Make us
clean. Help us to take care of each other in this
house.
Amen.

resources & actions

You

- Fill your home with cheerful music.
- Read and meditate on Psalm 98.

Family

- Purge entryways, closets, hooks, baskets, drop zones, and mail catchers together.

Group

- Read Revelation 3:20. To whom is Jesus speaking? If Jesus were actually coming over for a meal, how would you prepare for the visit, and what would you cook? Describe the setting and meal in your journal.
- Pray for each other.

journal

journal

journal

8.

Books

Are books a difficult category for you? I love my books and have kept quit a few children's books to read to my future grandchildren. There aren't a lot of things that I've kept from my children's childhoods, except books and a few sets of toys.

With having homeschooled for seventeen years, I had quite a large stockpile for every subject. I did manage to give away or sell a lot of curriculum over the years, but I still had textbooks and other things which were pricey and difficult to part with.

Last spring I began a book downsizing spree. It began with a homeschool group Book Swap which I volunteered to host at my home. It was a lot of work, but I did manage to sell hundreds of books. I didn't make a lot of money; I was more concerned with our beloved books going to good homes. It was a bittersweet time for me, as I was coming to terms with the finality of ending our homeschool journey. It took me three years of mentally and emotionally letting go to be able to finally close the door on that chapter of my life.

I still had too many books after the sale, but fortunately, the lady who sold us our puppy last summer is also a homeschooler and I sent her photos of books she might like. As a result, we did an exchange where I sent her heaps of books for a reduction in our puppy fees. It was a great exchange. I learned that even if I wasn't personally homeschooling any more, I could encourage and support others who are.

Could you also exchange books for other goods or services?

books to keep

Keep books you will read again, read to children, or loan to close friends. Also, keep books you use for study or reference on a regular basis, however, many study and reference books are now online, so every bookshelf does not need a massive Strong's Exhaustive Concordance of the entire Bible in King James English.

Consider space limitations and restrict books to your existing shelves so they are not overflowing on tables and floors. One minimalist I have seen will only keep ten books. When he buys a new one, he parts with an older one.

books to give

Give to others; it's a basic Christian principle. Give to a thrift shop, to the library, to your friends, family, and acquaintances. Also give to strangers. The knowledge we gain from books stays inside us, and we carry it around with us wherever we go. We can journal new knowledge or revelations as we read, as well as how a work affected us.

Begin a lending-library. My husband and his coworkers give and take from a small book stockpile at work. Some churches and groups have their own small libraries, so members can share resources.

People of faith know that everything we do is rooted in what we believe and has spiritual implications. When we give our books to those who need them, we write love on their hearts. We are showing that someone cares about them more than a precious book. If we need the book again, we can buy another copy. However, giving books to people who haven't asked for them is probably a bad idea. In addition, do not expect your mother to store your excess books in her basement indefinitely. That is simply avoiding the problem.

heart check

When we give to those in need, we are actually giving to Jesus. In this world we may acquire and love many things, but when we pass from this life to the next, we can't take any of those things with us: not one book, nor one piece of jewelry, or even one dollar.

God's ways tell us that it is better to store up treasure in Heaven where moths, rust, and thieves won't deplete our wealth. Instead we are to share: take care of the widows and orphans and give to those in need.

If you are having trouble sorting through belongings, it's safe to assume you live in one of the wealthiest countries on earth. One day we will stand before the Holy One and give an account of what we've done with all He's entrusted to us. We don't actually own what we have, but instead we are workers in God's vineyard. The entire vineyard belongs to Him, and we decide how to use and disperse the time, money, possessions, and influence He allows to come into our lives. I want to hear Him say that I was a good and faithful servant.

Sometimes I lie awake and feel bad because I know people who are not as well off as myself. Does God expect me to sell my home or invite them to live with us? Maybe. But God doesn't want us to make rash decisions. Instead He loves it when we pray and ask Him what to do, are faithful to do what He asks, and do it cheerfully. It isn't any good to be at a meeting and hear a preacher promise a miracle if you give a lot of money. I heard that once and I couldn't believe my ears. God isn't in the business of selling miracles, or His favor.

Watch your heart. Are you making bargains with God— if you give me this, I'll do that for you? It doesn't work that way. Here is how it works: be faithful to take care of your home and family; be faithful to give to God; give generously to the poor and widows, but do it all with thought, motivated by love. Also, consider the quality of items you give. If you have two maternity dresses, will you give the better one to an expectant mother in need?

It may seem unexpected to read all that in a section about downsizing your book collection, but I had on my mind the Bibles in my book collection. At one of my part time jobs before I began my own business, a lady picked up the Gideon Bible in the waiting room. She was going through a difficult time recovering from a workplace injury. She said she'd never read the Bible. I suggested she take it home and bring it back next time, so she did. The next time she came, I gave her a bible I'd brought from my shelf. She beamed. It made my heart sing, too, because there is much more joy in giving than in receiving.

The funny thing was that almost as soon as I took that job, I wanted to quit. It wasn't anything like I thought it would be and some unkind things happened. I tried hard to ignore those feelings and I decided to settle in. One day an old co-worker contacted me to offer me a job. I jumped at it, thinking it was my ticket out of there. Sadly, I was acting like Rebound Betty, going from one bad job to the next. I had to get out of that cycle, but how?

I had gone through some difficult things in the past, but as a middle-aged woman trying to find a good work situation, it was tough. I never knew until recently what it felt like to be pushed down, to be marginalized. It was painful. It gave me a new empathy. Personal pain can be unexpected and deep. When could I move on? I felt like Joseph, stuck in jail. What was God trying to teach me?

As for the lady and the Gideon Bible, I could see that despite being a Rebound Betty, going job to job in search of a place to settle, God put me there so I could love that lady who was going through a difficult time. God's mercy was with that woman. God is close to those who are suffering unjustly. God is right beside the brokenhearted. He sees those who are doing themselves harm as they try to cope with painful experiences and situations. His heart must ache for people; I know his body bled at Calvary when He was beaten, suffered with nails through his wrists, and hung on the torture device called a cross for you and me. Jesus knows what suffering is. He suffered for us.

When I look back over my own life and all the wrongs I've done, I am amazed that God forgave me and has accepted me. How can I be self-righteous and not forgive others?

Father God,
Thank You. I love You. Forgive me for hanging on to things and desiring more instead of considering

eternity and giving more generously. Help me to love others and find joy in giving to make their lives better. Thank You that You work Your good in our lives, regardless of our bad decisions. Heal the hurts others have done to me, Lord. Help me to forgive, just as You forgave me. Help me to stop rebounding in every direction and start listening to you.
Amen.

resources & actions

You

- Research free online books at Project Gutenburg and BookBub.
- Download the Overdrive App and link it to your Public Library so you can borrow ebooks.
- Listen to Psalm 1 with an audio Bible App.
- Journal about items you will give. Is giving difficult for you? Why or why not?

Family

- Go through your book collection and decide which books you'll give.

Group

- Read Luke 3:11 and Mathew 6:19. What are we to do with belongings?
- Read Job 1:6-12. Who allowed circumstances to come into Job's life that challenged him to grow in his faith? What does God show us through Job's life?
- What difficult circumstances are you facing?
- Pray for each other.

journal

journal

9.

Living & Family Rooms

The living and family rooms may be many different things to different people. To some, the living room is a formal reception room where they visit with guests and the family room is a place to watch movies or read while the children play with toys. Those are the usual uses of those rooms, but many families don't have two rooms. Most young families starting out have smaller homes with one main living room that must serve many purposes.

Remember, getting organized isn't about having a show home; rather it is about decluttering and being able to use your home for the priorities in your life. Personally, I like to be able to have friends in to my home without needing to spend eight hours cleaning. And while the things on my walls are for show, it is for the show I want myself and my family to see.

decorative items

It is important to display artwork and items that speak to our family. There are frames available for every budget to display children's art. Keep a large portfolio made of cardboard and rotate the displays. Try to keep only the Hall of Fame artwork, especially if your child is a budding artist who produces a lot.

Our daughter enjoys painting and over the years, we've displayed her watercolor paintings. Our older son made a small cannon in a metalwork class which we display on a window sill in the living room. And our young son has had principal roles in theatre productions so we display his group theatre photos.

And for my husband, I have on display a large poster sized frame with many small cut outs of fishing photos. I've included First Fish caught by each of our children, and some big ones by each of us, as well as friends. It sounds like a funny thing to have in our living room, but mainly it is the room where family gathers for a night in. The frame is narrow and black and the matting white so it has a sharp modern look, even with some vintage photos within. On our walls, I also have two framed prints of my favorite paintings, and another framed print my husband bought from an artist on a trip.

A living room should be personalized without being cluttered and busy. I am not a fan of knickknacks, although I have appreciated some beautiful displays in clients' homes. I am just not that committed to dusting. It creates too much mental clutter for me.

Other items which create mental clutter for some clients, are words which are visible. Signs with words, books, movies, calendars, posters, etc. Remove items you can part with; relegate the calendar to a desk or inside the pantry; cover books with plain coloured paper. Use a different colour for each type of books: green for travel books; yellow for cookbooks, etc. Another tactic is to use cardboard, wicker, wooden, or plastic holders. Doing so will augment the decorative aspect of your living space, so consider which materials will best go with your décor. Wicker lends an earthy feel; wood contributes to a crafty/homemade décor;

and colourful cardboard or plastic holders add a modern or whimsical touch.

use of space

Determine the main functions of your space and declutter. Keep table tops and shelf-tops clear, except for occasional use of baskets and holders as needed for storage. If possible, it is good to have enough seating for your own family, plus two extra spaces. If you have more people over, bring in dining room or folding chairs, unless your budget allow you to purchase multi-use pieces such as storage ottomans for occasional seating.

stations

If you happen to have a large living room serving many purposes, try to plan several "stations". Have shelves or baskets and pillows or bean bag chairs in a corner for a Reading Nook.

Make or find child-sized table and chairs for a Play or Craft Station in front the window, or near the kitchen for ease of cleanup. Coffee tables are great as multi-use furniture. Our large square

Ikea table is "antiqued" from all the child play over the years as it served well for Hot Wheels, blocks, colouring, and more. If you must have toys in the living/family room, everything must still have homes, even if in baskets under the coffee table or on a shelf. Baskets with lids are ideal or baskets that fit into a wall storage system. The low baskets work great for toys and books, while higher cubbies are for 'do not touch' items.

gifts

Over the years, friends and family have given us gifts to display. I was always appreciative for the kindness of the giver, but in all honesty, sometimes the gifts did not suit our home or tastes. I didn't have qualms about passing those things on, either to fundraisers or to a thrift shop.

I had to laugh one year, when I donated a quirky teapot to a school for their children's Candy Cane Lane sale. Each student was encouraged to shop among the donated items for family gifts. One day at a friend's for tea, she used the quirky teapot I'd donated. We had a good laugh about it, and she genuinely enjoys the gift her son chose for her.

That same friend brought a loud, speaking doll to a Christmas potluck at my house to use for our "Re-gift Exchange." We all had so much fun with the item. It brought much more fun than if she would have left it buried in a closet. The kindness of the giver is always treasured; the gift re-gifted can bring more joy.

heart check

A common challenge for family space is keeping it neat. Tidy every day for just a couple of minutes and enlist everyone to help. It's easier to complain about family members leaving items in living spaces than making sure everything has a home. I want people to be relaxed in our home and use it for living, but I should also help each person be accountable for cleaning up their own messes. If I am being lazy, I am not doing my job of helping them grow in their life skills. If I take the effort necessary to do my part and call them in to help with the tidying routines as participating family members, it will be much easier to maintain clean, tidy, welcoming living spaces for our family, and for our friends who visit.

When I think about the term living room, I think about what living actually means. Not simply existing, or getting by, but really living. God's word talks about Him giving us an abundant life. It could mean material provision, but much more importantly, it means riches that are unseen—gifts, talents, peace, joy—to name a few. Personally, I feel the most content when I am able to use my spiritual gifts and talents.

As a young believer, I was one writer on a team producing a newsletter. Years later, after a decade of freelance writing, I was the managing editor of the resurrected publication of the same name. I had an amazing team of professional editors, graphic artists, and writers. We produced a fantastic magazine for which I could not take much credit, since God had brought us all together.

I was also able to find outlets for my coordinating/administrative gifts by taking gradually more difficult roles, some volunteer and some paid, from nursery coordinator, homeschool group leader and event planner, to volunteer care coordinator, and administrative projects coordinator. At times I wouldn't have a clue how to proceed, yet the person who asked me had seen my gifts in action. I'd accept in a step of faith, and God showed up in surprising ways and gave me ideas with which to proceed.

I firmly believe that God puts people together in groups, whether churches, families, or other organizations, just as He plans. If we take the time to speak with people and get to know them, we will undoubtedly discover complementary abilities, gifts, and passions.

Of course there is no such thing as the perfect church, job, or family. As long as we live in a fallen world with imperfect people (myself included), there will be conflict, misunderstandings, and hurt. But that shouldn't stop us from trying.

Consider your gifts and how you are currently using them. Or are you using them? Sometimes it is difficult to find an outlet. However, whenever I faithfully pray and seek out opportunities, I can always find a way to help others and build up the church with my gifts.

Father God,

Help me to not be lazy, but do my part to ensure everything has a home in our house. Help me to make each family member feel special by displaying something they've made, or something they've chosen in our family living spaces. Thank You for the gifts people have given to us over the years to express their love. Bless them for their giving, and help me to be able to find new homes for the gifts I can't use; may they bring joy to others.

Thank you for the spiritual gifts you've given to me. Help me to discover opportunities to use them; connect me with others of similar gifts so we can build each other up; and may I learn to use them in a helpful way. May I not cause offense or conflict.

Amen

resources & actions

You

- What are your spiritual gifts? Do a gifts survey at your church or online: http://www.willowcreek.org/media/chicago/documents/spiritual_gifts_assessment.pdf

- Journal how you currently use your spiritual gifts, how you have in the past, and how you'd like to in the future.
- Journal about re-gifted items as a way to remember the kindness of the giver.

Family

- Allow your children to decide which of their items they'd like to re-gift. Do not make them feel guilty.

Group

- Bring an item to re-gift.
- Read 1 Corinthians 12:1-11. Where do spiritual gifts come from?
- Discuss your spiritual gifts and how you currently use them, or have in the past.
- Read Ephesians 4:9-19. What is the purpose of spiritual gifts? In the same passage, what are signs of immaturity and maturity?
- Pray for each other.

journal

journal

journal

journal

10.

Toys

Some popular organizing techniques are: bring in one toy, take out another; rotate toys weekly; toss any toys which are broken; give away or sell toys your children out-grow. All good ideas. But what if those simple ideas don't work?

It is overwhelming when entering a room and everything from Barbie clothing, Lego, Little People, puzzles, Play Doh, books, crayons, and usually lots of string, garbage and sticky things are all mixed together. It's enough to make a grown woman cry. And mothers do cry over these horrible messes which look like aliens from another galaxy. Some parents begin calling their children monsters, jokingly believing that their little darlings are in fact alien species concocting a spaceship so they can "go home". If only they'd take all their mess with them!

The first mistake adults make is letting children be boss of their toys. There is no way children should first of all have enough toys to build a space ship; and second of all, they should never have access to sticky things without supervision. Sigh.

Who authorized their spacecraft building anyway? NASA certainly did not. Their grandparents did not; well, maybe some of them would, if they are shopaholics who send an entire toy store for each monthly event. You may have noticed by now that this is a sticky topic for me. I have a huge aversion to out of control toys. Don't get me wrong— kids have toys, they will play, and they will make messes. That is normal and acceptable. I'm talking about extremes.

If you have well-meaning friends and relatives sending heaps of plastic every chance they get, you'll kindly need to ask them to start giving to starving children in developing countries. Hook them up with a Kiva account for their birthday, or adopt one or twenty Compassion or Feed The Hungry children for them, in their name. It's okay to not allow others to facilitate a state of chaos in your home.

toy rules

Rule 1: Everything needs a home.

Rule 2: Children may not have easy access to all their toys for dumping out of their containers.

Rule 3: Mom and Dad have the right to limit the number of toys out of their containers, at all times, and for all events.

It is a fact that children who clean up their own messes make far fewer messes, and messes of less magnitude. Some of you know what I mean. The opening description didn't begin to describe your children's rooms, playroom, and all the common rooms in the house. When your home is like that, your children will not respect their things; and they won't respect your things.

Take back your house. Take back ownership of the toys, of the rooms, of the lives of those little people who have been entrusted to you to help form good character.

It is also helpful to reduce the amount of toys we purchase for children. They don't need every toy invented. Do the children a favour and let them dream about that toy they want for a while. When they work and save up money to buy it themselves, they will be more careful.

Rotate toys: put some toys in storage so children are accustomed to a smaller quantity of toys out at one time. Doing so makes it easier when outgrown and broken toys need to leave the house. Using this strategy, I was able to donate toddler toys to a nursery. If you ask a young child if he'd like to part with his baby toys, he'll usually say 'no'. However, don't do this if it will cause trauma; wait until the child is ready to move on.

Consider proactive strategies, rather than reacting out of anger or resentment. Put together a plan. Kids thrive on routine, so using toy rotation and a chore chart based on life skills works wonders.

Life Skills

Ages 3 & 4

Help put away toys
Dress (with help)
Put clothes in hamper after undressing

Clear plate after meals
Help set the table
Brush teeth & wash face with help

Ages 4 & 5

Know full name, address, and phone number
How to make an emergency call
Easy dusting
Clear table
Feed pet
Learn about money
Help vacuum & sweep
Help tidy bedroom
Brush teeth, comb hair, and wash without help
Put clean clothes away
Help sort laundry
Choose clothes to wear

Ages 6 & 7

Empty dishwasher
Help cook & bake: mix, stir, and cut
Help vacuum & sweep
Make a basic meal: sandwich, salad, soup

Help put away groceries
Use basic household cleaners
Straighten the bathroom
Straighten bedroom
Make bed
Bathe unsupervised

Ages 8 & 9

Load dishwasher
Wash pots & pans
Fold clothes
Care for outdoor toys
Take care of personal hygiene
Use a broom and dustpan properly
Dust bedroom
Vacuum bedroom
Mop bedroom floor
Read recipe & prepare a simple meal
Help create a grocery list
Count and make change
Answer the phone & door
Lawn & garden work
Take out trash & recycling

Ages 10 – 13

Stay home alone
Go to the store and make purchases
Change own bed sheets
Vacuum several rooms
Mops floors well
Clean bathroom thoroughly
Use the washing machine & dryer
Plan & prepare a meal
Broil & bake foods
Read labels
Iron clothes
Sew on a button
Sew clothing tear
Apply knee patches
Learn to use basic hand tools
Mow the lawn
Babysit younger children

Ages 14 – 18

Research careers
Clean stove & oven
Vacuum & change bag

Fill a car with gas, add air to and change a tire
Understand medicine labels and dosages
Interview for and get a job
Learn to drive
Maintain a bank account
Prepare and cook meals
Navigation with GPS & maps
Paint interior & exterior

Young Adult

Make regular health appointments
Learn to budget finances
Learn about investing & credit
Pay bills
Understand contracts & leases
Basic car maintenance

heart check

Why have we allowed our children to have the run of the house and trash things? Or why don't we train them to help clean up? True confession time: when I was a young parent, I felt overwhelmed by my children's toys. Before I learned the rules I listed above by seeing how others managed toys, I too often let my kids make a mess. I'd be too tired to do much about it so I left the house messy for days and weeks. And when it came time to clean up, it was easier to do it myself than to get them to help.

Eventually, I knew I had to train them to help. It was for their own good. I couldn't allow them to keep going in that direction since it was too disorganized for us all.

A larger issue related to toys is the misplaced focus on possessions over time playing with our children. Parenting experts agree that children want the attention of their parents far more than material possessions. How can we declutter our homes and lives to make more time for each other?

This section may seem overwhelming. Don't give up. It takes a while to implement a new system. When you do get chores figured out and a system going, there may be times when you give up. That's okay. In fact, you may elect to do chores on just one or two days a week if it's easier for your family. However you decide to manage your children, know that taking a break doesn't mean giving in or giving up. You may re-start whenever needed as many times as needed, until your children grow up and move out. Your reward will be the work your children do.

If you do purge and implement a new tidy system but still find toys to be a problem, purge more toys. Also, consider storing all the toys in a pantry with a door, or a locking storage unit and allowing children to "borrow" only one or two items at once.

Father God,
Please forgive me for allowing our children to create unchecked messes in our home. Please give us your wisdom and perseverance to teach life skills so they value their belongings and take care of all You've given us. Help us to say no when it's in our children's best interest. Show us how to shift focus to place greater value on time with each other over possessions.
Amen.

resources & actions

You

- Read, *Shepherding A Child's Heart*, Tedd Tripp.
- Journal.

Family

- Create a Chore Chart for the whole family or one per child. Research ideas on Pinterest; decide on rewards such as one-on-one time with a parent or the choice of game for Family Night.
- Spend one-on-one time with each child and cultivate close relationships.

Group

- Read Proverbs 22:6. What does it mean, '...in the way they should go...'?
- Pray together specifically for each child, and for your families as you implement chore charts.

journal

journal

journal

11.

Papers

Paper in North America poses a huge challenge. How can we stem the flow of paper to our homes? In this chapter I will address what to do with paper when it arrives, how to keep it, what to keep, and finally, how to safely discard paper with sensitive information.

keeping files

Keep tax records: Personal and business financial records should be kept for seven years. Check your local tax rules, as some jurisdictions allow for electronic files.

Keep documents: Health and insurance records, passports, birth certificates, marriage license and certificate, death certificates, diplomas, awards, degrees.

Discard: Monthly bills and statements for investments should all be available electronically.

Convert to electronic: For those who have businesses, you do need to keep financial records, but work toward using electronic systems which will make record keeping streamlined and eliminate the need for a large hardcopy filing system.

In order for an electronic method to work, we need to educate ourselves on how to use computer filing and record-keeping effectively. Alternatively, take a course at the local college. Learn how to create Folders and place appropriate electronic copies inside each Folder. You may also scan hardcopy documents to add to the electronic files. Afterwards, shred paper copies. Advanced MS Word courses will also teach methods to simplify document creation and storage.

Numbered systems are only necessary for large records systems in most cases. Small businesses and families do best with an alphabetized system.

Discard (most) manuals: All manuals may be recycled as (almost) everything is online. And when was the last time you read a manual to learn how to operate a new device? Most people play around with the equipment until they figure it out.

However, having worked in an office with a complicated photocopy/fax machine, it's best to keep some manuals and actually refer to them as needed. But you could check to see if there is an online version if you are striving for a paperless office.

Safe Storage: Rent a safety deposit box at a bank or use a fireproof safe. Most if not all of these documents can be replaced at your government service center, so a simple filing cabinet or drawer insert in a desk will do fine.

Recycle and Shred: Papers and files without sensitive information may be recycled. Paper with personal information including full names and address should be shredded, or at the very least, blacked out with a permanent marker.

Shredders are affordable for most people. It is best to shred papers and old files regularly, so your shredding bin doesn't become too full to handle. If you have never shredded or purged any of your files, you may want to hire a professional service with an industrial shredder as it may take as long as a week to shred a large volume. In the past I burned out a shredder which needed to be replaced. Now with my new shredder, I try my best to shred discards weekly.

Any necessary hardcopy files, kept either in a filing cabinet or desk drawer with a file folder hanger, should be put into alphabetical order by the company name, or by its purpose name. Here is a list of common household files: Achievements, Automobile, Documents, Health Care, House, School, Taxes.

Some clients prefer to break files down further into the type of car they drive, a file for each person which will contain all their birth and health records, separate files for each insurance provider, files for every investment. Ideally, there should be a Master List at the front, itemizing the contents, in case of sudden death, making the executor's duties less cumbersome.

If you convert entirely to electronic files, create a Document Master List with passwords. Email it to someone you trust, or to your executor. It should include the names of all your financial accounts, investments, health records, PDFs of deeds and other documents, etc.

paper flow

Paper flow to the home needs to be controlled. When you retrieve mail, sort before you get inside the house and deposit junk mail and flyers in to the paper recycle bin. Flyers are all online. Keep one or two for your husband's reading if it will keep him happy.

Inside the house, put mail into one of two dividers in a paper sorter: Needs Attention or File. For papers needing attention, be sure to put them in order of dates. Look at the Due Dates of when action must be taken. Schedule Action Items on your calendar, several days or weeks beforehand, or both. Use a computer or phone calendar, and check it daily. If you don't have time to complete a scheduled task, move it to the next day, but be sure to check your Mail Sorter daily to keep up on what you must do.

The section of your sorter which is Filing should be dealt with daily or, at minimum, weekly.

school papers

Papers sent home for parents from school may be sorted with the mail. Put them in the sorter as Needs Attention or Filing. For papers your child must deal with (assignments, homework, projects), have a place for your child to keep them all together, and deal with before due dates. Help him to schedule them on a calendar, and be responsible for his own work, as his maturity and abilities allow.

The main rule is to not let paper pile up. It makes the pile feel overwhelming and the more daunting it looks, the longer you will put off digging into it, and dealing with things.

Sometimes people lose their papers and as a result, don't pay bills on time. They get into all sorts of difficult situations because they haven't dealt with their paper. One business owner I know has told me his business is in danger of failing because he is so behind in his paper work. In a case like that we may ask, are unseen forces causing his business to fail? Some people have a bad attitude about The System when their focus needs to be on organizing their own papers.

children's artwork

One of the best ways to store children's art is to have a large, cardboard portfolio inexpensively purchased at stores such as Staples. For smaller art, a table-top file sorter works well, or an Art Box. For prolific artists, try to limit what you keep to Hall of Fame or Gallery pieces, as mentioned earlier. Ask them to choose their favorite work.

For artwork which does not lie flat, display for a while and then take photos and print off, then add to their art portfolio. Or keep art photos on a zip-drive or hard-drive.

As a culmination of a childhood full of art creations, consider having a book printed of the images, or simply create a virtual book to share through email or a social media site.

heart check

By procrastinating with paper work, am I putting our family's credit score, business, or anything else at risk? Am I encouraging a sustainable lifestyle? Our lives need to be balanced between work, family, self-care, worship. Do I include all in my weekly calendar?

When I was stressed during my Rebound Betty days, there didn't seem to be anything that would permanently help me to feel relaxed. My family had left one church and began attending a new one. It did help as it was a better fit theologically, yet it was difficult to leave behind church family.

I exercised, I tried massage, therapeutic essential oils, vitamin supplements, and they all had limited, temporary relief from stress. During that time, I watched a teaching series about the life of Joseph.

Joseph's time in prison resonated with me. He had a chance to get out. He had told the baker he was unjustly there. But for whatever reason, God did not allow that information to result in Joseph being freed. God had his own agenda. He let Joseph learn a valuable heart lesson while he was serving the other prisoners in jail. His prideful heart had been exposed and we see how Joseph was pointing his finger at the wrong others had done to him.

That is exactly how I felt at times. Through that series, God showed me my self-righteous pride. By then I was ready to hear the truth, as painful as it was. It was the only thing that brought me permanent relief. I sought God's forgiveness for my self-righteousness, and I forgave those who had wronged me. The stress in my life began to dissipate.

Father God,
Help me to live a balanced life and encourage my family to live balanced lives, too, teaching each to be responsible for their own work. Help us to have sustainable lives— enough rest and self care, time for recreation, time to spend with You to build our relationship. Where we are out of balance, help us to seek balance. If we are holding pride, self righteousness, or unforgiveness, help us to forgive and seek forgiveness.
Amen

resources & actions

You

- Set up online banking, bill payments, statements, and electronic business practices where possible.
- Organize and properly store children's art work.
- Journal.

Family

- Recycle manuals and general files.
- Shred old documents with private information.
- Read the Bible account of Joseph's life together, a little each day, (Genesis 37:1-47-27).

Group

- Discuss the lessons of Joseph's life.
- Revisit Genesis 45:4-5. What did Joseph reveal as God's over-arching plan?

- Can you see narratives of struggle and purpose in lives around you, and the church in general?
- Pray for each other.

journal

journal

journal

12.

Technology

It's incredible to consider the rapid multiplication of electronics in households over the previous decades, from one TV and wall phone per family, to many devices. Some, myself included, would argue that it hasn't been a positive development.

To organize all your tech devices, use tape or a label machine and label your cords, chargers, and anything else which may get separated and lost. Keep all the cords and chargers together. Some clients utilize a desk drawer with dividers; others keep a container on a shelf in a storage room.

Recycle all the packages and papers, manuals and instructions that come with your devices. Everything you ever wanted to know about your devices including how to use them is online, usually in videos anyone can follow. The key is doing an effective search: type exactly what you need into the search bar.

The challenges around tech devices are affording expensive services and regulating screen time. I've had an eye opener recently while my phone was broken. I managed to get by without it quite well. I used Messenger and email to speak with family, friends, and business clients just once or twice a day on our desktop computer. I pondered eliminating my cell phone permanently. If I did, I could save almost a thousand dollars every year. Is it sustainable?

I realized just how much time I had spent checking email, texting, and scanning social media sites when my working phone was in hand. I'd click on quite a few stories and get lost in an avalanche of random information. It is good to be informed, but where do we draw the line?

Most articles, blog posts, and pieces written for online magazines and business sites are biased. For any opinion represented, there is an equally valid opposing view. Professional writers and journalists are vetted through the editors and publishers who employ fact checkers. Be wary of where you information is coming from. Look at who the publisher is. Who funds the work? Trace back to the source to find the slant. While many posts are interesting, not all have true value.

heart check

Do we have tech devices and services which we can easily afford, or are we trying to keep up with our friends? How can we reduce our charges to make our lifestyle more sustainable?

What are we reading or viewing, and would we be embarrassed if our family saw? How much time do we spend staring at screens? Excessive screen time and anxiety have been linked in research.

After I left one part time job, I went back to work at a place where a friend had offered me a job. This time, I would split my time between full days in the front office, as well as part time weekends out in the field. The weekdays in the office were spent on projects. I created reports, organized files, offices, and periodicals. I also reorganized electronic files. I was able to work independently and bring my own skill and ideas to the projects. I found I enjoyed the work and it was satisfying. The year before, when trying to find my purpose, I had briefly looked at becoming an organizer, but the idea felt overwhelming. I didn't know much about starting a business.

One year later, finally, something rang true as I continued to read about organizing from many sources, and worked on organizing my own home. There emerged the bright ribbon of organizing things, places, people, files, and more throughout my adult life. I was more organized in my own life and home than ever before. I was seeking a simpler life; one where I was no longer Rebound Betty, no longer grasping for validation from others about my identity and worth. God was doing a work in my heart, reassuring me He's already chosen me and made me his own; He has completely forgiven my past, present, and future failures, and He loves me anyway; He calls me his daughter; I am royalty to him. I don't need to rely on others for a job any more. I would create my own job. I would start my own business and help other people.

I read books on starting my own business and I completed Professional Organizer training online. Technology is wonderful when used right. Once the idea stuck, it really stuck! It gave me energy and focus. I no longer felt conflicted about all the things I'd tried and programs I'd not finished. I could see how all the things I'd learned informed this new venture. I had taken courses in Business, Communications, Ministry, Leadership, and now Organizing. What a beautiful blend it turned into, as all provided me the tools I need to succeed with the business.

Lord,
Thank You that I don't need cell service to keep in touch with you! You have said that I can be content in any and all circumstances. Help me eliminate whatever I can and cut back on my time online so I can have more time with You, more time with my family, and more time with people who I can help. I want to be fully present in other's lives.
Help me to be aware that anyone can write anything; give me your discernment to know what is true. Thank You for all the ways technology has made life and a future more accessible to me. I love you, Father!
Amen.

resources & actions

You

- Read *Timelock*, by Ralph Keyes.
- Send a real letter to someone special.
- Limit online time to one slot in the morning and another in the later afternoon/evening, leaving the nighttime free to unwind and build relationship with family.
- Journal.

Family

- Enlist help sorting out cords and devices.
- Recycle unused devices.
- Choose one day a week to unplug together.

Group

- Discuss social media. Do you think it helps foster better relationships?
- Read 1 Corinthians 12:12-30. Is every believer a member of God's Body?
- Read Genesis 1. In Whose image are we created? What implications does that

realization have for you? Are all people created in God's image?

- Pray for each other to use technology wisely.

journal

journal

journal

13.

The Master Bedroom

This is the one room in the house where husband and wife can be alone. It should be a calm, attractive, intimate sanctuary. I suggest that it's best to make it appealing to him, as well as you. What husband wants to sleep in a room that looks like a little girl's room? Aim for sophistication and grownup colours.

Never use the master bedroom for a dumping ground, extra storage space for random junk, office space, an exercise room with bulky equipment, or any of the other ways people try to multi-service the space. You should also not allow your husband's collection of sports memorabilia or gaming junk to litter shelves.

Keep the wall art simple, tasteful and grownup, just one or two pieces which you wouldn't be embarrassed about if your mother-in-law has to pop into the washroom on occasion. Choose window coverings for complete darkness and privacy, and the nicest, softest bedding you can afford. Keep the table tops and dresser uncluttered. No photos of relatives. Who wants to feel like others are in the room? It is also not recommended to have mirrors facing the bed.

What to do if you feel you have nowhere else to move the office equipment or extra items requiring storage? Sell, donate, or recycle them. Put simply, that is a sure sign you have way too much stuff. Remove all the clutter, even if you need to pack it all into Banker's Boxes for now. Take it to a different area of the home and plan a day to go through the contents and decide what to do with it all. There is no excuse to have an office in the bedroom anymore, since most can afford an inexpensive laptop with Bluetooth capable hardware to use in the living or dining room. Commit to making the Master Bedroom a special place for the two of you, in honor of your marriage.

master closet

Once the main area is finished, tackle the closet and master bath, if you have one. Use the same method as with the children's clothing. Take everything out of the closet and go through it piece by piece, deciding what to keep and what can go. Avoid having a "Think About" or "Undecided" box since that prolongs the process. By now you should be really good at making decisions. Hang as many clothing items as possible.

Purses and shoes may be kept in boxes on the floor or on shelves. Purge all items that you haven't used recently. Try to be ruthless.

Decide which section is His, and which is Hers. Group winter coats, jackets, dresses, sweaters, skirts, pants, long sleeved tops, short sleeved tops, sleeveless, and tank tops with thin straps last. Next you may hang a section of night wear, exercise wear, or any other special category. Fold casual pants including jeans, fleece and yoga pants, and place them on the shelves above the rod. Some unique categories may be: plaids, special occasions, suits, costumes, sportswear.

You should own a few drawers at least, for each person. The drawers may be in a dresser or part of the closet organizer. They may be used to hold underwear, bras, stockings, socks, and swimwear. Bras are best placed sideways nested together. Other items may be rolled or bunched so all are visible. Drawer dividers may be used to separate items, but they spread items out so that more drawers are needed.

Consider your own space and downsize your wardrobe if it doesn't fit into your storage space. Be realistic about your current lifestyle and the clothes you wear. Being generous and giving good quality items is commendable. Some people won't give away expensive items. There is no reason to waste clothing this way. An item is used wisely when it is worn, not just hung in a closet to collect dust or as a monument to a past lifestyle or income bracket. Old suits and dresses often look outdated and need to be replaced when a mother returns to work anyway. If we have two suits and someone has none, we need to be willing to part with one.

Once you've downsized, rather than continuing to overbuy with the thought that your discarded clothing will go to charity each year, try to make do with your current wardrobe. Redirect those funds toward lifting a woman out of poverty in a developing country.

jewelry

If you have unused gold or silver jewelry, consider selling it to a jeweler. Some jewelry stores are owned by craftsman who buy and reuse precious metals and gems to form new pieces. Give peices to relatives or friends as gifts. When you purchase new pieces or know you will receive an item as a gift, consider buying jewelry from a social justice project and literally be adorned with good works.

Organize costume and precious jewelry in boxes, drawers, or or on hangers and hooks on the backs of doors or on a closet wall.

master bath

Keep the master bath, if you have one, clean and tidy so you and your husband can enjoy time there away from the children. How long are medications and makeup okay to store? Check expiration dates when available.

Toiletries Storage Guide

2 years: Hair care products; shaving cream; tooth paste, nail polish; deodorant, mouth wash, soaps
18 months to 2 years: powders
1 year: creams & lotions
1 year: lipstick
6 months: lip gloss
3 to 4 months: mascara & liquid eyeliner
7 weeks: Sponges

Purge items in doubt of expiration date, and items you don't use. Do not give old toiletries away.

heart check

This chapter may make you uncomfortable if you are having any difficulties in your marriage. Let me assure you that God cares. He especially cares about marriage because He is the One who thought of it. Marriage on earth between one husband and one wife is a picture of Christ and the Church. He loves and cares for us, and is making us sweet and pretty, pure and holy, for when we meet at the Wedding Feast.

Looking back, despite all my personal struggles, my husband has been a rock. He and I were both unbelievers when we met and married, and he didn't get to know Jesus until seventeen years later. Regardless, he had a more stable upbringing and supported me, adding logic to my creativity and emotion. God often puts two opposite types of people together because together we make a great team.

Early in my marriage, I reached a place where I wanted to quit. There was nothing really wrong with our relationship; I just felt empty inside. My husband did his best to hang on while I floundered. Not long after, a co-worker shared the gospel with me. I remembered Jesus from church as a kid, and from the time when I was a teen. A classmate asked if I knew Who Jesus was. I answered, "God's Son". I learned that God, even though He is holy, wanted a relationship with me. And the way to begin a close relationship with Him was to ask Him to forgive my sins. Nothing else.

I prayed with my co-worker and God lit up my heart and life. I was transformed from being spiritually dead to being alive in Christ. I had a hunger for Him, and a passion to tell everyone about the amazing gift of eternal life.

At first, my new faith caused conflict in my marriage. Gradually, I learned how to less obnoxious and more loving. Jesus made my marriage stronger.

God's plan is perfect for our lives. It is messy and difficult finding the right path at times, but even challenging times are valuable for healing, growing, and learning to have deeper faith. We will never stop learning and growing if we allow God into every area of our lives.

Father God,
Thank You for my spouse. Bless our marriage. May it be honouring to You. Help us to cherish each other. Help my husband to know how to love me. Help me to know how to respect him. I trust You to help us with anything that is difficult right now. Help me to be an example of giving and serving. Be the centre of our world.
Amen

resources & actions

You

- Read books, website, and blog by Sheila Wray Gregoire: www.sheilawraygregoire.com.
- Journal a prayer for your marriage.
- Return the toilet seat to the "up" position for your husband.

Family

- If your husband is willing, attend a marriage retreat together, or plan one yourselves.
- If you are having serious problems, go to marriage counseling.
- Read 1 Corinthians 13 together. Create a poster or write it on a chalkboard or whiteboard.
- Consider how to give a mother in a developing country a hand up with vocational training or business funding through Compassion or Kiva.

Group

- Skip group time this week and go on a date with your spouse. If you are a single parent, take turns taking your children out for a special breakfast or activity.

journal

journal

14.

Your Partner's Stuff

Just as your belongings may be sentimental to you, so will your husband's be to him. Earlier I mentioned a pressure cooker my husband was attached to. He's much more sentimental about things than I. He has several collections. I have learned to leave them alone; I just move them to appropriate storage places. Over the years, those collections have become amusingly vintage.

I was able to get rid of my college books long before he could. In fact, I think he still has his. Does he use them? No. I keep working on him; every year I ask about them, when I declutter.

Since beginning my organizing business, my husband has been much better about keeping his garage organized. I have offered to help him, but he's resisted, instead taking it as a cue to tidy up. (He may secretly worry that I will declutter *for* him.)

Very seldom have I gotten rid of anything belonging to my husband without asking him. (I did toss a few pieces of clothing damaged beyond use.) He is his own person and I shouldn't nag and ridicule him to change.

There are times I have bought clothing for him; perfectly nice shirts and more, but if they aren't items he likes, he won't wear them. It doesn't matter how attractive or expensive they were. I've learned over the years to leave him be. He shops at the same store he did when I met him. He is solid and steady; a man I can always count on.

Offer to help your husband, but don't force it. Be his biggest fan, not his critic. No one likes to listen to an annoying ticking noise. That's what a person sounds like when there are constant little complaints.

I believe God calls us to encourage and build each other up. Take time to notice all the things your husband does well. Consider information earlier in the book, such as Love Languages and spiritual gifts; identify how you differ but compliment each other.

If you are in a place where you are stuck, where you don't know which way is up, when you don't know any more what the purpose is to your life, don't give up. Keep working through your home and possessions and look for the connecting dots. Practice with your husband's things. What are the things he bought and kept all these years? Are they related to his accomplishments over several decades? Sometimes it is easier to connect the dots for others than for ourselves.

Now look back over your own life. Can you think of times in each decade of your life where you accomplished something you were proud of? What was it?

Accomplishment Assignment

Make a list of three to five accomplishments for each decade of your life.

What did you do that you felt good about?

Did others affirm your achievement?

How did you work? By yourself or with others? Are you more task or relationship oriented?

Do you like a definite start and finish?

Do you like to take the lead, or let others lead?

Write down as many details as possible, to help you understand how you like to work.

Finally, add a "why" for each accomplishment. Why did you do those things?

heart check

Chances are, if you are feeling unsettled and stuck, it is bothering your spouse. Be gentle on him. Don't expect him to solve the problem for you, but do allow him to help if he has suggestions. Remember he can't read your mind. Help him to help you and if he gets it wrong, don't be angry with him. At least he's trying.

When I was trying to find permanent work, I felt pressured by my own desire to succeed. I also felt pressure from my husband to help bring home some of the bacon. It all came to a boiling point one day. I could not manage working full time, plus take care of our home and be a good mother. I was receiving some help from family members, but not enough to sustain full time work outside the home. I had to admit my limitations, and reign in the type of work I could do, and the hours I'd be available. I resigned from my job and began to look for a new one. Now what? I asked God. I had to let go of the resentment which had been brewing. I had to accept who I was, the amount of family contributions, and what I could realistically do.

Father God,
Thank You for my husband. Where there has been hurt, please bring healing. Help us both to forgive each other and stay committed to making our marriage work. Help me to be a wife of noble character, using what I have without sacrificing what is important. Where we have held wrong priorities, such as work and possessions over family, help us to have Your wisdom to adjust. Thank you that You, Who created the whole universe with Your word, are able to meet all our needs with the riches of Christ Jesus.
Amen

resources & actions

You

- Find creative ways to display your husband's collections, especially his achievements.
- Journal a list of accomplishments for your husband and yourself.

- Read Proverbs 31.

Family

- Discuss your Accomplishment Assignment with your spouse or children. Ask for feedback to help you pinpoint specifics that can help you discover the types of work and situations that you find motivating.
- Revisit your priorities. How should they inform your quest for purpose?

Group

- Discuss your Accomplishment Assignment with your group.
- Discuss Proverbs 31. Could a woman do all those things in one season of life? Discuss how this psalm may be the progression of a woman's life.
- Pray for each other.

journal

journal

journal

journal

15.

Photos

Photos are the hard stuff. Why are photos so difficult? Every little snap is a time capsule. It is exhausting to relive many years' worth of experiences in one sitting. During a photo purging session over one week, my twenty years of photos took me from morning until late each night to sort. I was physically and emotionally drained each day.

Many of our joint memories were wonderful and I gladly relived them, like our wedding day, when our babies were born, fun trips. But what wasn't recorded were the subtexts of our thoughts and feelings in between or even under the photo snaps. There were periods when we were going through rough patches. Seeing the past only through the lens of the camera, distances us from the realities, but our bodies and minds have stored the emotions of the moments, the hours, the days, and the years.

How to store photos and the important memories and events of our lives is a personal choice that will vary for each family. At the start of our marriage, I kept photo albums for every year. Yet now, with so many digital images, I have had very few impressions printed. One of my family's favorite albums is a scrap-booked family history put together by my sister-in-law. She made copies of photos from as far back as she could find. The album includes a family tree.

Photos from the early 1900s were family poses in front of houses, at a studio, or in front of a college or other important building. However, as photography became more accessible photos became more plentiful. There are pictures of grandma at Blackpool; an image of Uncle Jack playing billiards at the neighbourhood pub. Regardless, it only took the one album to documents three generations.

I want to return to that. To construct one album for each of our children that will hold those same photos, with just a dozen or so more from babyhood up to adulthood. And when they are married with their children, they will copy the photos and add their own few monumental impressions, single moments in time, documenting the expansion of the family tree. Or so I hope.

With old images, it is best to scan them and create digital images to do away with the bulk of photos in boxes. There are many businesses who can do this for you for a reasonable price. Use what you can of the printed images to create albums, but limit them to one per person, if possible. Additionally, zip drives loaded with photos may be plugged into electronic photo frames to scroll through display images. They are a great, compact way to enjoy photos.

Many women are into scrapbooking which I have tried. It took me an entire afternoon to create one page of an album. It took another week to finish the project. I am not a fan. I think scrapbooking overcomplicates the photo keeping process, unless one is able to do it in a way that is less art project, and more archival.

If you must scrapbook, keep it simple. An alternative is to use an online photo site to have books printed. It is a little pricey, but the finished product can be stunning. Or, as previously mentioned, keep photos electronically and share via email or social media. Take the necessary time to either store photos on the Cloud, or make several copies and keep in different locations.

If you come across photos which you don't know what to do with because they include people from your past, allow yourself to consider throwing the photos away. Throwing the photos away does not mean you are throwing away people or the experiences as even difficult times are useful to help us grow. So keep what you would like to keep and consider how tossing the rest may be therapeutic for you. In any case, if photos are buried in a box somewhere in your basement, it isn't as though they are serving a constructive purpose in your life. Toss them and see if that helps you feel lighter.

For those who have experienced divorce, be kind to your children and include a wedding photo in their albums, even if you choose not to keep any for yourself.

Personally, I have discarded all scenery photos (without people), as better images are available online.

heart check

In the case of people who are no longer in our lives due to death, divorce or estrangement, consider what is happening in your heart as you handle the photos. Sometimes there is unforgiveness, bitterness, or a sadness that is holding on to us tightly, and we can't move on.

First, forgive where forgiveness is needed. We forgive others not because they deserve it, but because God asks us to. We must to live our lives as whole people. One of those people is my father. He was a harsh parent, and I was afraid of him. To this day, if someone displays anger, I cringe. I am overly sensitive to vocal tones. However, I still love my father and I have forgiven him. I wrote him a letter once, explaining how I felt, and telling him I forgive him.

Consider all the things you have done in your life which may have hurt someone else. No matter how bad it was, God offers you his unconditional forgiveness. In the case of abuse, even that we can forgive with God's help. We can never enact justice on them, or teach them not to behave in those horrible ways again, but God is able to, so hand the person over to God and believe that He will work. Don't think you have to tell God what to do; he sees all and knows all. He saw what happened, and he is grieved for you. He will handle it with His righteousness and goodness.

Heavenly Father,
Thank You for being here with me. Help me to be healed and free from the past. Make a new way forward where I can live a new life. Cut off my past and graft me in to Your everlasting family tree. I love you, Lord; I choose You. You promise to bless up to a thousand generations the families of those who love You. Bless me and my family. May we do Your will and help Your kingdom to come. And I lift up to you those who have abused. Have mercy on them; help them to stop hurting others, and grant them repentance.
Amen.

resources & actions

You

- Add to your journal. List things you are thankful for, as well as your current projects and dates you'd like them to be complete.
- Research biographies and notice which photos of a person's life are included. Try to reduce your photo collection to major events.
- If you are having difficulty time letting go of past hurt and abuses, seek out a counselor; ask God to heal you.
- If you have gone through a tragedy such as death or divorce, find a support group or begin one.
- Journal a letter to someone from your life who has passed or moved-on to help you through the grieving process.

Family

- Schedule photo projects on a calendar and work on them together.
- Write real letters together.

Group

- Bring and show any completed photo projects to your group.
- Read Romans 8. Discuss the difference between the sin nature and life through the Spirit. What kind of relationship has God called us to? How should this affect our lives?
- Pray for each other.

journal

journal

journal

16.

Keepsakes

Keepsakes are often the most difficult items to deal with. Now is the time to consider what is truly valuable, how much space and time you'd like to commit to keepsakes, and how you'd like to display them.

A great product to use for each child is a dedicated School Years Keepsake Book, with one small section for each grade, from Preschool to Grade 12. There is a place for a school photo and a pocket for samples of work. It is compact and efficient. Coupled with one photo album each, even a large family will have a manageable collection.

My own family has an affinity to the ocean. On one of our trips, we took a photo of our older son along the oceanfront, the wind blowing his hair. It was a rocky shoreline and from there, I brought home a handful of smooth stones, all different sizes and colours. The image is mounted in a shadow box with the stones and a few shells.

Another keepsake project I undertook was to use my husband's old jeans to make a quilt. I'm not a serious quilter, but I discovered that I could make a simplified version of the log cabin design without too much trouble.

Discover your own keepsake themes and projects. Research what others have done with their collections; gather ideas and do something about it. Schedule regular time to tackle these projects until all your projects are complete.

If you feel overwhelmed, either reduce the number of keepsake projects, or give away and recycle the items. I once kept another quilting project in a Project Basket for several years. Whenever I saw it, I'd feel stress. Finally, I gave it to a thrift shop. It eliminated the stress, plus provided a ready-to-do craft project to someone who had time. I never looked back. In fact, that experience helped me to continue giving even sentimental things more freely.

I am not very sentimental about most things, but I am about my wedding dress. I have chosen to keep it hanging in my closet where I see it. I can enjoy the fabric, the patterns, the textures any day I chose to dwell on it. The few things I want to emphasize and promote in this life are marriage and family. I believe they are very dear to our Heavenly Father.

Our keepsakes should not be so many that we cannot appreciate them. If there are mountains of clothing, toys, books, knickknacks, mementos, plaques, badges, certificates, etc., how will anyone take the time to weed through that mountain to find the treasure? Sort and choose only the best and discard the rest.

Some of my clients have a lot of things they don't want to part with. When we discuss why, we discover the items are tied to happier times in their lives. What many fail to realize is that the past easily becomes shrouded in nostalgia. By anchoring hearts in the past, it becomes increasingly difficult to be happy in the present, and that dissatisfaction often fuels negative behavior which further exacerbates the problem. Is there a way to appreciate the past, it's happy memories and lessons, without creating a shrine? For younger wives, it's best to practice letting go of things which will become crucial as the family grows and passes through difficulties; even perhaps floods and fires. We cannot see into the future, but keeping our eyes on Jesus and on the intangible things such as love, relationships, and our faith, we can throw off whatever might hinder us.

heart check

Do you have things which anchor your heart to the past? Are you having a difficult time moving in to the future which seems unsure? Know that the God who made you also loves you and wants you to have an abundant life. God isn't mean and vindictive. He isn't out to get you and make you have a miserable life. Also God is in control, so where you may feel uncertain about the future, God is certain. He is the Creator of the universe and He loves you. Put your trust in him, not in the past. Keep a couple of things if you must, or better yet, give them to someone who needs them more than you.

As I look through the few photos that exist of me at a younger age, only one as a baby and one as a child, I am reminded of who I was at those times. When I was a child, I loved to colour and draw. My favorite Christmas gift one year was a colouring book and set of crayons, with the highlight being the most divine shade of turquoise. I took my work to Show & Tell at school. As a teen, I loved painting best in all the art classes at high school. Those classes were the highlight of my life, even as my family fell apart and I ended up in foster care.

A few keepsakes reminded me of my friend Anita from my teen years. She was a fantastic friend who stuck by me when I went into foster care because my parents had divorced and my mother couldn't care for us. Anita's parents included me on family outings. When I moved out west, Anita kept in touch for years, encouraging me with my writing and art. Throughout my teen years, I wrote stories and poetry, short pieces for the high school newspaper, and I began several novels.

My current path had taken me far from writing and art. How could I find my way back to a more creative life? I parted with most of my keepsakes, but the memories and skills are still with me.

Father God,

I love You! You created the Heavens and the Earth. You are the beginning and the end. You know everything that will happen before it happens. You are in complete control of everything, and nothing happens which You don't know about. Why do people die and leave us when they are young? Why do people get abused? Why do people die of cancer? Why are innocents hurt? For some reason, You have chosen to give us free will. Some use their free will wrongly. But even that You can take and turn around and use for good in our lives, and for others. Make good things come of my life. You number our days. For the ones you have taken after a short time, I believe they accomplished what You sent them to do. You are the Potter, we are the clay. Every day is a gift which has a purpose. Each day, let me help someone whether in person or through my work. Make me useful to You, Lord.

Amen.

resources & actions

You

- Journal a record of keepsakes you will part with, as a way to remember them.

Family

- Purge keepsakes until they are manageable.
- Research display methods for your keepsakes with each family member. Schedule them on your calendar.

Group

- Read Psalm 103 and 2 Corinthians 5. Discuss God's benefits toward us. What kind of ministry has God given to us? What is the difference between our earthly dwelling and our heavenly dwelling to come?
- Pray for each other.

journal

journal

journal

journal

17.

Shopping

With all the purging, no doubt there will be thoughts of replacing discarded and donated items. As I purged my clothing, I realized many items didn't fit, some I didn't like, and still more that I loved and wore often had worn out. I advise clients to begin a list of items they need. When a birthday or Christmas rolls around and your family and friends ask what you'd like, your list will be ready.

It will also be tempting as you downsize the contents of your home and get rid of clutter, to fill your house back up with new clutter. Try to resist the urge. The purpose of doing the hard work of processing the past, curbing the clutter, dealing with your heart, and getting to a calm, peaceful state, isn't so you can go shopping. In our culture, shopping is a hobby which offers a temporary distraction during difficult times. It's like putting a Band-Aid on a migraine headache.

As you purge and eliminate old belongings, live with the clear surfaces, the uncluttered bookshelves, the lighter house for a while. Enjoy feeling lighter. If you don't feel a sense of lightness, you need to pray and ask God what is causing the heaviness and holding you back from moving forward. Most likely you haven't purged enough.

Quickly go through the house again, looking for more items to sell, donate, or trash. Keep purging until you feel lighter. A well-purged home will be easy to keep tidy. That is a good evaluation tool.

Another aspect which I haven't mentioned yet, is the financial side of things. Many people shop using credit and get into financial trouble. If you have an unsustainable shopping habit, shred your credit cards and replace with the prepaid variety. Pay them off, and get your financial life on track.

heart check

My mother was a person who struggled with illness and owned very little. She lived simply and didn't ask for anything. Our last visit with her as a family was a trip to Niagara Falls and Marineland. She was tickled to see my baby son, and quietly delighted in seeing my healthy, happy children and husband. When she died of cancer a few years later, my sisters and I were at her bedside, and we sang hymns with the angels to usher her into Heaven. I believe in Heaven she'll have a mansion if she cares to have one. She sacrificed continually for her six children when we were little. Her marriage fell apart and she was left with nothing, but she wasn't bitter. She left me no financial inheritance, but she left me an example and fond memories. She demonstrated contentment in every situation. She was resourceful and did the best she could with her limitations.

People usually know what is holding them back but don't want to face it. Are you angry at God about your situation? Do you think life has been unfair to you?

Are you limiting yourself from growing because you don't think you deserve it, or does it seem like too much work to change? Is fear holding you back? Consider whether or not you have forgiven yourself for your past decisions. Every day is a new beginning. You are the only one holding yourself back from experiencing an abundant life. God has already said he wants to give you one.

Father God,

Show me how I need to change my relationship to shopping and possessions. Give me Your strength to continue purging and organizing. I am weak, but You are strong. Help me to be content in whatever situation I find myself, whether with a lot or with little. Fill my heart with thankfulness, and help me to praise Your name, even though I don't understand some of the really difficult things that have happened. You see all, know all, and are in charge. Help me to trust that You are working Your good.

Amen.

resources & actions

You

- Journal. Are you finding contentment in your situation? List that for which you are thankful.
- Read, *From Dream to Destiny—The Ten Tests You Must Go Through to Fulfill God's Purpose for Your Life*, Robert Morris.

186

- Unsubscribe from online shopping sites. Trust that when you need to buy something, you will be able to find it at a good price.
- Do not go to garage sales, rummage sales, thrift shops, etc., unless you have a shopping list of needed items in hand. Stick to your list; don't impulse buy.

Family

- Read financial books such as: *The Wealthy Barber*, David Chilton; *The Storehouse Principle*, Al Jandl and Van Crouch; and *Debt Free Forever*, Gail Van-Oxlade.
- Use Gail Van-Oxlade's free website tools to create a budget together.

Group

- Read and discuss Colossians 1. What kind of inheritance does God have for us? Describe God's involvement in creating the world and sustaining it. Where should we direct our energy?
- What were your biggest challenges this week?

- Pray for each other.

journal

.

journal

journal

18.

Find Your Keys

Finding your keys ALL THE TIME is the litmus test to your whole new organized life.

A common solution is to have a key holder with hooks by the door. Hang them every time, and you will always be able to find them. The reality, however, is that when we enter our homes, nine out of ten times we have full arms and we can't dig for our keys to hang them, or we forget, or we are rushing inside to soothe a baby or make it to the bathroom while potty training. The best solution is to pay attention to where you dump the contents of your arms. Usually, it is in the kitchen on the counter, or on a table in the hallway.

Place a decorative bowl, basket, or key hanger where you usually dump your keys; place another bowl at the second location. When it's time to retrieve your keys, you'll have just two locations to check.

Part of the problem is our hectic society. We equate tight schedules and busyness with importance, status, and success. Try to shift your thinking if you struggle in this area. Begin to relate an uncluttered space and life with having a more calm, focused, productive life. It may mean removing more belongings and activities from your life, to provide more family time, and more intimate time with God.

When we make quiet times of worship priority, God's Spirit fills us with calm and contentment. We can't consistently come into His presence without being changed in a good way. He is alive and well. He's the ruler of the universe and He cares for us.

How much time do you spend alone with God? If possible, set up a prayer closet in a quiet part of the house where you can go to be alone. If space doesn't allow for alone time, designate a chair in the living room with a table for your Bible, journal, a candle, and your study books. Tell your family that when the candle is lit, you are spending quiet time with God. Children soon learn to allow mum a little special time. To be fair, limit your time to ten minutes when children are little, up to half an hour to an hour as the children grow older. This quiet time is as necessary as drinking water. Without it, your faith will be parched. As you seek God, He will meet you. It is one of the great 'keys' of an abundant life.

heart check

One of the most difficult times for me was when our oldest left for college. She'd homeschooled right through high school and did some college through distance education. To top it off, she had a gap year at home while she worked to save for college. I grieved for about six months after we drove her to college one province away. At the time, my young son said, "And where do you plan to drop me off?" with a stricken look on his face. It did seem cruel. She was crying, I was crying, and my husband was crying. The boys were upset too, but they hid it better.

That time was a wake-up call for me. I realized I had invested in a vibrant relationship with my daughter, but I hadn't invested as much into my friendships with my sons or even my husband.

Eventually, all our kids would move out, so we had to learn how to be a couple again.

Additionally, I wasn't trusting God to help me move past the difficult transition. It's easy to say we trust God, but what does that look like? When we experience loss, we will grieve, but our grief as believers should be different: our grief should be tempered with faith in the unseen, all-knowing, all-loving sovereign God. When we take Him our emptiness, He fills it with a peace we can't understand.

For six months, I did what was necessary to care for my family but I lacked passion and purpose. Finally, I turned off the television, got up, deliberately spent more time with God, and made a mental list of things I'd enjoyed in the past. I forced myself to begin writing again. I prayed for and took on more volunteer work, and I found a part time job. When I embraced the new season, God open doors and used my gifts. I felt whole again.

resources & actions

You

- Read Philippians 4:1-7.
- Journal a record of your personal losses for which you've grieved or are grieving.
- Decide on a quiet time and place for each day. Set this example for your family.

Family

- Consider having a Bible reading time each day as a family. You could use a devotional book, an audio Bible, or switch things up occasionally to include short teaching videos.

Group

- Read Revelation 1:17-18 and discuss Jesus' keys. What do they represent? How did Jesus acquire them and what do they signify about the future? How does this hope affect your heart?
- Share the highlights about your week.
- Pray for each other.

journal

journal

journal

journal

19.

Pulling It All Together

It takes less effort to do a little each day than to let the house completely go and have to dig out from under an avalanche. Tackling a giant mess takes more mental will power, since everyone has a point at which the volume becomes overwhelming.

The main tools used throughout the book are: purging to reduce belongings, and organizing to create appropriate homes for keepers which are in line with our priorities. Next, consider systems. Systems already mentioned are: paper, toys, chore charts, and drop zones. In this chapter I will add laundry and cleaning, plus scheduling and goal setting.

laundry

Every system requires effort. Let's consider the habit, or system of throwing clothes on the floor. At first it appears that this takes no effort at all. However, the owner will have the inconvenience of living in a messy space which makes every day more stressful looking for things. When laundry day comes, it's a large project to gather everything together, wash and dry the items, and put them away.

People who are organized spend a little energy most days on laundry. They take off their clothes at night, re-hang clean-enough items to wear again, and put laundry directly into a hamper. Generally, people who do this have a different place to hang wear-again clothes either on hooks, on a chair, on top of a piece of furniture, or one section of the closet. As time goes on their room is fairly neat: just the airing clothes and their growing laundry pile. When their hamper has enough for a load of laundry, they pop it into the washing machine, never letting the laundry pile up to the point where it takes hours and hours. Laundry becomes a small, quick daily or weekly chore, taking minimal effort since each person in the family will usually have no more than one week's worth of clothing.

Having less clothing definitely helps to reduce the volume of laundry. Also, doing it often helps to keep it under control. Personally, I worked out two separate systems: When I had young children and I was responsible for all the laundry. I used one laundry basket for each person, lined up on the laundry room floor. I also used a laundry sorter with three sections: whites, darks, and colors. As I pulled items out of the dryer, I folded them and placed them into the appropriate person's basket. Baskets went to bedrooms and the clothing was put away into drawers and closets. I would aim to do one load a day. As the children grew older, they took over their own laundry, but I asked that they fill up the washer with items from the sorter, mainly towels and bedding.

Now that I only do mine and my husband's clothes, I no longer need the basket system. As I pull items from the dryer, I will either lay them flat on top of the dryer to be hung, or fold and place into a pile for drawers. I then take the piles and put away; the flat items are put on the bed and I add hangers before moving them into the closet. It takes almost no time at all. I do the bedding about twice a month, more often in the summer.

The best laundry setup I've seen is to have a washer/dryer right in a large walk in closet where clothing and linens are kept. Second best is a laundry room next to the bedrooms. If space allows, some large families keep all the clothing in the laundry room and children retrieve their outfits which are hung by size on rods, for one or two days at a time. Soiled clothing is returned to a sorter.

Confession: socks have been a sore point for me. I try to pair them as they come out of the dryer, but what do you do when you put two in and one comes out?

cleaning

For ideas on keeping the house clean and maintained, consider Chapter 10 Life Skills training for children and even adults. Set goals for each person to learn a new skill, such as repairing clothes, caring for a pet, or car maintenance. Goals and chore charts may be updated quarterly, bi-annually, or yearly. In a family with several children, it is crucial to train the oldest and the younger ones will usually follow. Consistency is key.

My housework load was the lightest when I had two trained tweens. We lived in a bi-level house at the time; each would tidy, dust, and vacuum one level of the house. I would clean the bathrooms and wash floors with my young son, and everyone helped with daily dishes and laundry. It wasn't perfect, but cleaning about once a week was satisfactory for us.

If your priorities keep you busy and house cleaning isn't one of them, consider hiring a cleaner as often as your budget allows. Keeping a house and family well organized is a big job. If everything is put away, a cleaner takes far less time to come in and do the heavy cleaning. Here is another opportunity to exchange services or to work with a friend. I was once part of a cooperative of mothers who deep cleaned each others' homes. The idea was to provide motivation and companionship to each other.

family goals & schedule

When priorities are identified, include them on your schedule. Work with your husband and children. Though it may sound difficult to attain, try to leave about one third of your time unscheduled. This allows for surprises and emergencies, or added downtime which we all need.

What about one solid day at home with nothing scheduled? For those who attend church on Sundays, Saturday is the logical day off. Try to keep groceries, laundry, children's activities, and everything else to the other days of the week, even if it means missing one practice.

For homeschooling families, make mornings at home a priority for children to complete their lessons, especially for older children. Afternoons, evenings and weekends work well for clubs, volunteer work, and more. Each family will be different and every year will need some adjusting.

Our family soon discovered that there were more opportunities for our children than we could schedule or afford. While each child had lessons in swimming, skating, and skiing, once they had the basics we did those activities together as a family and chose not to pursue competitive levels which required travel. I also required our children to take five years of music lessons as we were aiming for well-rounded children. This comes back to goals.

Consider individual goals when scheduling your family.

There are different seasons in life and priorities will change. Each year reassess and develop a family schedule in line with individual and family goals.

Examples of goals for children:
Learning to read, manners, keeping bedroom tidy, completing chores without complaining. Secure a part time job, etc.

Examples of goals for a family:
Family fun activity every Saturday to build relationships. Sunday family dinner together with adult children each week, even when they live out on their own. A family mission, such as working with Habitat for Humanity, an annual trip to help a missionary or orphanage, or helping local single parent families with car and home maintenance.

heart check

Transition times are often difficult for women. Gradually, as I continued to pray and ask

God what I should do, He revealed to me the bright ribbon of organizing which wove through every part of my adult life. I enjoy using the gifts God has given me because I am able to help people make positive changes. In addition, my past achievements had elements which I am able to utilize. Have you discovered new elements about yourself as you've worked through your home? I discovered I like a definite start and finish to a project to feel a sense of accomplishment. I am able to be creative with aspects of the business, as well as work collaboratively in each home I visit, being sensitive to clients' individual needs.

Before beginning my business, I discussed it with my family to make sure it resonated with them. Being successful in our priorities will require support from family members. As an example, my husband often cooks on weekends to allow time for me to pursue my writing and artistic goals. It's taken a while, but I've discovered when I use my creative gifts, I am tapping into the joy in my relationship with God. I feel His joy.

Other times, I enjoy God when I am relaxing in a quiet room or outside on a walk; not doing, but just being. He tells us to come and drink from Living Waters so we don't thirst. God really does care about us. Every aspect of who we are, what we do, and how we live. He sees the mess of junk in the basement and garage, and He still loves us. He sees the disaster which has accumulated in the pantry, and He still loves us.

As a young mother, there were times when I was exhausted. We were all sick and the house was a disaster. Suggesting you get organized isn't a judgement on living and coping with what comes your way. It's saying, life will go better if everything has a home and tidying up will go better, when you can. There is always grace with God.

Those times when I was weak, I cried out to God and He filled me with His love and strength. Sometimes I'd cry and complain to Him, and He'd speak into my heart His love, reassuring me. He gently leads mothers with young ones.

For older women, I hope you are excited that God does have a purpose for you. You are never too old to serve the Lord, and definitely not too old to enjoy Him! Part of life is about what we are to do, but our deepest fulfillment comes from knowing who we are and being connected to God in a vibrant relationship.

need help?

If you feel stressed out in your home because it is too cluttered and you just cannot tackle it, even with this guide, you need to enlist help. Professional Organizers can help you make a dramatic change in a short time. You could schedule a weekly appointment and tackle one area at a time. Or have her help with the worst areas. Working with her will provide motivation and training for you. Make sure to ask questions. What are her rates? When is she available? How does she like to work—room by room, or category by category? Does she offer any discounts or have any special offers? Some organizers will reduce your final bill in exchange for the use of Before & After Photos, plus a review for her website. It doesn't hurt to ask.

If you cannot afford an organizer, ask a friend to work with you and offer to help her in exchange. Working together makes a big difference with motivation.

Our modern society isolates us. We are told to be independent, fearless, and wildly successful. However, we all go through times we can't manage alone during which we come up with all sorts of coping mechanisms.

Sometimes women use shopping as therapy. Sometimes women buy things as a way to hurt their husbands or compensate for devastating loss. Sometimes women hang onto things as a way to keep the past alive, robbing themselves of living in the present. Some seem to insulate themselves from painful experiences with nice things. Sometimes women give up and don't maintain their homes, allowing all sorts of items to get mixed up and piled together as a quiet rebellion. And for some, their lives are busy and the house takes low priority.

Life is hard. We suffer alone in a barricade of possessions that have ultimately let us down. Objects, no matter how nice, regardless of the good memories and happy feelings they may activate when we hold them, are not alive.

Possessions cannot heal, insulate, love us or keep us company. Keeping others' possessions cannot bring them back or keep them near. Rather, they become tombstones blocking us from living. When an object no longer has a purpose in our lives, even if it was a gift, by giving it away we are allowing it to bless another person. When we give, we are taking good care of our homes, our lives, other people, our world. Giving is much better than receiving. God is pleased with our giving.

When I was young, we didn't have much. I believed the lie that having a lot of nice belongings would make me more acceptable to others. I looked for romantic love and approval from people. As a people pleaser, I did things as a teen I regret. I had a boyfriend, because I thought that meant I was acceptable. One thing led to another, and I found myself pregnant at 17. The thought of becoming a parent so young caused a lot of stress in my life. I was losing weight and suffered with migraine headaches when I was pregnant. Finally, a doctor suggested I consider giving the baby up for adoption. It seemed like a good solution at the time.

I had no idea how to care for a baby, so I agreed. I felt an older couple who were stable financially could provide a better home. It was one of the most painful times in my life. I felt like my heart had been ripped out. A while later, I gave my life to God, and I began to pray for the little girl I didn't know. I regretted giving her up for adoption, but it was too late.

Eventually, I decided it was time to find the girl. My family agreed, but before I could locate her, a friend had found her for me. The past collided with the present, and I met her. She is a beautiful young lady. My biggest fear was that she'd hate and resent me. Instead, she understood that I'd made the best decision I could at the time. I'm thankful we've met and we have a relationship now. We see each other once in a while, and keep in touch.

Before she and I were reunited, I carried around a lot of guilt and shame over my past. I rarely told others about her, because I thought I would be judged. I hid her, and regretted my past. God has brought healing and restoration to that part of my life. He is a good God, turning our ashes into something beautiful. Since then, I've been able to talk about adoption as being a good alternative to abortion for unwed mothers. After one talk, news reached me that a young lady had decided to keep her baby. I was in awe of how God used me to save a life.

We must be lovingly honest with ourselves and others if we really want to get unstuck and find our purpose. At every stage in life, no matter how difficult a situation may be, God is there. It does take effort; sometimes a lot as with this past season of my life. I did finally find purpose helping others through my work, yet my true peace and joy comes simply from enjoying my relationship with God.

God, You are my Father,
I love You! Thank You that You love me, too. Life is hard, but You know that. Send Your Holy Spirit to fill my heart and comfort me when I am weak. Help me to be as gracious with myself and others as You are with me. Help me to set the right priorities in my life, and make time for them. Guide me in making practical choices about possessions my family needs. Help me to be content in whatever situation I find myself. You are here; I am never alone.
Amen.

resources & actions

You

- Create a personal calendar if you don't already have one. Use an electronic one if possible.
- Journal as part of your quiet time each day.

Family

- Develop a list of goals annually for each family member, and one or two family goals.
- Create chore charts if you haven't already.
- Create a family calendar. With young children, it's best to use a paper one displayed where it is visible to everyone.
- Schedule time for your Photo and Keepsake projects.

Group

- Start a cleaning co-op if the idea appeals to you.
- Read, *A Shepherd Looks At The 23rd Psalm*, W. Phillip Keller. Discuss God's extravagant care for us.

journal

journal

journal

journal

journal

20.

A Plan For The Future

Did you find a bright ribbon? Nothing in the past is wasted. Everything I have done in the past, every job and volunteer position, as well as my work at home with my family have made me who I am today. We can't always work in a perfect position, but in any job we can work hard, do more than expected, and have a great attitude. Some women may impact a large number of people at once; others will impact one life at a time as they live humble, caring lives.

In whatever situation we find ourselves, we can aim to make good use of our time by studying, improving gifts, and growing in character. As we do so, our gifts will improve. Those who faithfully use their gifts will serve with the attention of kings. More importantly, we serve the King of kings.

If you loved the adventure of organizing your own home and life as well as your family, consider training to become a Professional

Organizer. The profession is in demand and the hours are flexible. Personally, I am able to prioritize family over work, and keep to school hours.

If you are challenged by this journey because you are unorganized, don't despair. Keep trying, as anyone can learn and improve. As with any journey, we will stumble along before gaining victory. It is normal. Like David who stumbled many times but got back up again, we too should never give up.

Remember that being organized isn't about having a perfect home, or a show home. A home is for living in and loving in. Things get messy. Seasons with young children, valleys of loss, and transitions will be overwhelming. You will be okay. Those times will get easier, and you'll be able to make headway.

Keep working with your family: train the children to help, purge regularly, and be willing to give to those in need. Whatever I have given, God has always returned equal or more back into my hands.

For many years, our family prioritized home educating our children. I worked as a freelance writer and made a small, additional income which covered piano lessons. For a short time, I was able to secure a part-time facilitator position in a college. It was a great bonus. Regardless of my limited financial contributions, we were never without hearty meals, sufficient clothing, or a good home. Put God first and He will provide.

If you discovered you may have a serious problem because you were unable to make any progress in parting with possessions, do not be anxious about it. I pray God will bless you, heal you, strengthen you, comfort you, guide your steps, and help you find kind souls to assist you. Don't be afraid or ashamed to seek help.

In my organizing business, I receive referrals from a behavioral psychologist who has helped people prepare for change. In turn, I refer clients to her who are not yet ready to part with possessions. There is hope and help available.

Don't forget to look for the Big Picture. Consider how this point in your life is just one moment of time, and in many years, you may have grandchildren and great-grandchildren to love. Our society often ignores or mocks the elderly, but many studies show that living in a close-knit, multi-generational family and community is the healthiest situation of all.

A paid position, while good, may not be the best use of your time. Ask God to bring opportunities and ideas into your life of how to be part of a Big Picture family and community.

Father God,
Thank You that You do have a plan for me and for my family. Help me to know what work I am to do, but also help me to prioritize my family and enjoy You. Thank you that You have the victory and I don't have to live in fear or despair. Whatever I do, help me to honor You in it. And I thank You for the challenges that help me to grow. Give me Your wisdom to seek help when I need I, and strength to be a humble servant for You.
Amen

love song

At times, all the pieces of the puzzle are there—we know our gifts, our strengths, how we work best, and our homes and hearts are in order—yet we feel we are in a holding pattern. If that is your situation, this could simply be a test of faith. Use the time as a chance to go deeper with God.

Practice the art of savoring the moment. Slow down and relax. Special moments are tucked into each day yet we miss them if we are too busy or too inwardly focused. They may be a hug, a kind word, a stunning sunset, encouragement, a song, a pleasant atmosphere, a performance, the way the sunshine hits the wood on the floor—anything. Those moments are love songs from God. Furthermore, He sends others—people, angels, and His Holy Spirit—to minister to us.

Practice the art of thankfulness. Appreciate others. Add to your Journal all the moments which take your breath away.

I once had the goal to record five hundred thankfulness entries in a blog. It began with superficial observations, like toast, tea, sunshine, but eventually I dug deeper and recognized difficulties as experiences for which I was thankful. For example, a sickness gave me time to read, failure to find a suitable job led me to begin my own business. It's all a matter of perspective.

Your next assignment will come. It may take time as there are likely other people and components involved that need to get to the same place as you. Expect a surprise, because often, God will call us to use the same gifts, but in a fresh way.

As I write this final chapter, I am spending more time enjoying creating poetry, stories, and art. Some of my work has found publication and I feel a sense of God's blessing on that part of my life. In other ways, our family is struggling as we grapple with the needs of a relative. God has a way of allowing joy to mingle with heartache, so we can bear up under it.

Through our quiet times, in small groups of friends, journaling, and savouring moments of God's love, we can reflect on the process of life. There is continual movement and change. However and wherever you find yourself, know that you will be okay, and you are loved. Listen for your love song from God.

connect

How did you do finding your keys and figuring out life? I'd love to hear from you. Find me on Facebook or Twitter and tell me about your journey.

Group

- Celebrate to wrap up this journey. Do not buy anything for the celebration.

227

Epilogue

Just before this book went to publication, Fort McMurray the city where my husband and I lived for over 30 years, experienced a mass evacuation due to a fast-moving wildfire.

We had an indefinite amount of time to pack while we listened to the radio. When we were ready to evacuate, we'd packed just a few small suitcases, drinking water and laptops, a few important papers, and our pets. Rather than jam-pack our cars, we realized it was just stuff that could be replaced.

What began as a small fire, would explode into a raging inferno, nicknamed, The Beast. It grew until it consumed vast forests, homes, businesses, and threatened our livelihoods.

Throughout the challenge of being evacuated from our home on short notice, my family recalled what was truly important: each other. In fact, approximately 90,000 souls made it out through scorching flames, thick smoke, a congested highway, and exhaustion. All the evacuees, my family included, were deeply moved by the kindness of family, friends, and complete strangers.

People supplied free gas, water, snacks, and in the larger centres, clothing, bedding, gift cards, discounts, free services, free accommodations, and too many other things to mention. It was an amazing testament to God caring for the displaced through the hands, feet, and heart of people.

I marvel at the timing, how God so thoroughly trained my family in letting go of material goods through my work as an organizer.

The experience taught me to sympathize more deeply with people grieving over possessions, however, as so many lost homes including their keepsakes, photos, and more. It was a traumatizing experience for my family without overwhelming loss; how much more so for those who had only an ash-heap waiting in place of their homes.

As with all things in life, balance is the key. We don't worship our possessions—not houses, or cars, or keepsakes—but we thank God for His provision.

It was a trial, during which I was challenged to grow in my faith. God reminded me that He would provide for all our needs, even if we lost our home, even if our main source of income ceased. At times, the stress would press in on all sides, and God's Holy Spirit would softly beckon me to praise Him still. Then the cloud would lift, and His peace would come.

He is the God of the storm; He is the God of the celebration. I agree with Job, who said something like: Though He slay me, yet will I trust Him; yet will I hope in Him alone.

acknowledgements

I'd like to acknowledge those who helped to breathe life into these words.

First and foremost, my Lord and Savior, Jesus Christ. He took a quiet mousey me, from a rough background, and he made me into a lady (with a few less rough edges). He healed all the broken places and filled me up with His grace and Holy Spirit. Though I am always weak and fragile, He is strong for me. I love Him exponentially. When I sat down to write a novel during NaNoWriMo, the Lord had other ideas and gave me this work instead. He continually astonishes me.

I also want to acknowledge my first readers and editors—

Cyndy, for your gentle, loving spirit, and your encouragement. You set an example by living godliness in a busy family.

Diane, for your meticulous attention to detail and challenge to dig deeper into my heart. I appreciate your insight and honesty.

The Word Guild, for your prayer support and patiently answering my questions and helping me accomplish the daunting task of making this work available to others in the hopes it will help someone.

My NaNoWriMo writing group for creating time and space to write.

And thank you to my family who understands my call to write down words, even words about them—

Garrett, my sweet, creative, funny son who shines like a star every day. You remind me that God is an artist because He made you unique.

Aaron, my older son with a big heart, walking strong with the Lord. Your steadfast faith and love for people inspires me.

Chloe, my sweet girl: Thank you for reading all these words and suggesting edits. You are lovely, sensitive, loyal, and sweet. You challenge me to care and serve like you.

Jeff, my smart, funny, discerning husband, who loves me through mess and clean, chaos and order. You are the best husband God could have given me.

Elizabeth, my prayer warrior sister, for your support, and the example of your strong faith in our Mighty God.

Special mention to Chantal, my beautiful birth-daughter who has allowed me to include her story. Everything *does* happen for a reason.

Made in the USA
San Bernardino, CA
27 September 2016